Advance Praise for *Rare Breed*

"You have a choice to make—become a Rare Breed, someone who cares enough to contribute, to speak up, and to challenge convention. Not to hustle, which is selfish, but to make a ruckus and to make things better. Take what you need from this brazen rant and go!"

—Seth Godin, *New York Times* bestselling author of *This Is Marketing* and *What to Do When It's Your Turn*

"*Rare Breed* is a guide for strategic rebellion. If you're looking to make a difference in your business or in the world at large, wow, have you ever found the right book. Reading it will inspire you into taking big, immediate, spirited action."

—Mark Levy, founder of Levy Innovation and creator of Your Big Sexy Idea®

"In a business world that's a vast sea of sameness, you've got to be different—really different—to stand out and get noticed. In *Rare Breed,* marketing experts Sunny Bonnell and Ashleigh Hansberger provide readers with a radical guide for how to be different from all the rest and to draw like-minded customers to your company and products in droves. Read this book, and you too will learn the secrets of Rare Breed leaders—the men and women who do things differently, earn our attention and admiration, and make a real difference in the world."

—Peter Economy, *The Wall Street Journal* bestselling author and the Leadership Guy at Inc.com

"Entrepreneurs need to know how to really cut through the noise these days in order to grow their business. Sunny and Ashleigh's book can help by showing them how so-called vices are actually positive building blocks toward success."

—Michael A. Smith, producer at Bloomberg

"A good dish doesn't always start with a recipe, but with excellent ingredients, vision, and confidence. In this book, through the passionate and talented writers Sunny Bonnell and Ashleigh Hansberger, you will find all the ingredients that shape the path of many successful individuals in their craft."

—Daniel Boulud, renowned French chef,
James Beard Awardee, and restaurateur

"To all my Rare Breeds reading this: understand this book isn't a blueprint to success, as we all have to walk our own paths. But it will give you the strength to keep pushing because it's a beautiful reminder that you are not alone."

—Charlamagne Tha God, *New York Times*
bestselling author of *Black Privilege*

RARE BREED

HarperOne
An Imprint of HarperCollins*Publishers*

RARE BREED

A GUIDE TO SUCCESS FOR THE DEFIANT, DANGEROUS, AND DIFFERENT

SUNNY BONNELL
ASHLEIGH HANSBERGER

HarperOne

HarperCollins books may be purchased for educational, business, or sales promotional use. For information, please email the Special Markets Department at SPsales@harpercollins.com.

FIRST EDITION

Designed by William Ruoto

Library of Congress Cataloging-in-Publication Data

Names: Bonnell, Sunny, author | Hansberger, Ashleigh, author.
Title: Rare breed : a guide to success for the defiant, dangerous, and different / Sunny Bonnell and Ashleigh Hansberger.
Description: First edition. | New York, NY : HarperOne, 2019
Identifiers: LCCN 2019006113 | ISBN 9780062856937 (hardcover)
Subjects: LCSH: Success in business. | Success.
Classification: LCC HF5386 .B65 2019 | DDC 650.1—dc23 LC record available at https://lccn.loc.gov/2019006113

---

19 20 21 22 23 LSC 10 9 8 7 6 5 4 3 2 1

For Danny & Crystal Bonnell,

two Rare Breeds who taught us to own who we are

CONTENTS

READ THIS FIRST!

None of us were meant to be common. We were born to be comets.

—Donovan Livingston,
Harvard Graduate School of Education Convocation, 2016

It was early 2007. Motto, our young branding agency, had seemed like a comet when we'd launched two years earlier. Now it looked more like a meteorite about to burn up on reentry. But first, let's tell you how we got there.

We met as teens in the mid-1990s, back when AOL was cool—strangers who crossed icicles during a snowball fight in the suburbs of Chicago. Our chance encounter felt like two supernovas colliding in the cold air. Neither of us could've imagined how that big bang would affect our future. We had each spent our childhood marching to the beat of our own drum, and it was life-changing to find someone who moved through life in the same way. In those screechy, dial-up-modem "You've got mail" days, we saw the other as a magical portal from our humdrum, small-town lives.

One thing we had in common: entrepreneurship. It ran in our blood. Both our fathers and grandfathers had grown humble businesses from nothing into huge successes. From an early age, we witnessed the extreme highs and lows of running a company. We had ringside seats to their individual accomplishments, failures, leadership styles, and financial challenges, and ultimately, the sacrifices they made. Little did we know we would follow a similar path.

Young and bright-eyed, we embarked on the traditional path and enrolled in college together. Sunny, a musician all her life, shifted gears to follow her dream of becoming a veterinarian. Ashleigh graduated high school early at age seventeen and wound up in the English department in hopes of being a journalist. As a side hustle, we moonlighted with graphic design, creating gig posters and album artwork for bands, learning the craft on our own.

Still, it made no sense for us to drop out of college in our early twenties, just shy of our degrees, to launch a branding agency with $250 and zero experience, right?

So that's *exactly* what we did.

We called our agency Motto. A motto is a short statement that encapsulates the beliefs of a person or organization—it's a war cry. The name had symbolic significance and communicated the kind of company we wanted to build.

From the beginning, we were swimming against a rip current of doubt. People said we were too young, too female, too inexperienced, and too broke to succeed in a world where sixtyish admen made the rules. The only ones in our corner were our parents, and even they had worried eyes.

Who could blame them? Despite Sunny going back to school while running the business—this time with a scholarship to Savannah College of Art and Design—all we had was an audacious vision.

We started looking for role models in our industry, but the blueprint in our small, South Carolina town was old-school advertising agencies run by the old guard. We studied their work, and the more we learned, the less inspired we were. It was tired, static, homogenized, and templated. These guys were established, but slow and self-congratulatory. They moved like molasses, not like Jagger. They were big, impressive balloons, and we were sharp knives. So, with a motto stolen from Charles Bukowski—"What matters most is how well you walk through the fire"—we set out to change the conversation.

The ink on our business cards had barely dried before we started throwing haymakers at industry tradition. Other agencies worked out of lavish office suites; we set up shop in a shady part of town, in a tiny room inside an industrial warehouse. They had investors; we rolled pennies. They had hundreds of clients; we had none. We knew businesses were desperate for a different approach to branding. We just had to prove it.

There was just one problem . . . no one knew who we were.

To survive, we needed a Hail Mary.

It came in the form of a six-by-nine-inch paper garbage can. In an era when Yellow Page ads were all the rage, we spent the only money we had on a direct mailer. We designed it to look and feel like a galvanized metal garbage can, and when you pulled the lid the copy read "Trash the Ordinary" in a handwritten font with our phone number and web address. Nothing else. It was weird and it was brave. After getting our hands on a mailing list of nearby businesses, we mailed each one a copy . . . and held our breath.

Over the next several days, the phone started ringing, and people started showing up at Motto with the can in hand. We earned our first client: an ahead-of-the-curve dentist who wanted to, in his own words, "do something different." Together, we created an experience-rich, cutting-edge dental brand, a one-of-a-kind in our area. That success marked the first of many disruptions across traditionally unsexy categories such as law, real estate, audiology, hospitality, and food and beverage.

If it could be challenged, we would declare war on the ordinary.

After we won various competitions, earned some awards, and received copious amounts of national press, people got curious. Who were these young "girls" running an unorthodox agency from a warehouse in the ghetto?

Business-as-usual pushed back, *hard*. If you've ever lived in a small town, you'll understand. Small towns are notoriously locked down by established players. We had *no clue* we were a threat.

The big agency in town invited us to their office to try to size us up. They wanted our take on a campaign they were developing for a local bank. Everyone there had a leather briefcase. And there we were, at the far end of a table the size of a small country, feeling very out of place . . . with no briefcases. The creative director flung the work down in front of us. "What do you girls think?" We paused, all eyeballs on us.

Ashleigh: "Hmm, isn't this Target's tagline?"

Sunny: "Do people really care if they get a free blender with a checking account?"

Just like that, the meeting was over.

Yep, they had us escorted out. The CEO flung the door open and said, "You'll never be successful in this town."

After a while, we started to keep score:

- → Times we were sabotaged? **Sixteen.**
- → Times we got fired for the exact reason we were hired? **Twenty.**
- → Times we were told our ideas were absurd? **Hundreds.**
- → Times we were written off? **Thousands.**

We were learning the hard way that vision, dangerous thinking, and defiance of the status quo come with a price. It made the first several years of building Motto a monstrous roller coaster. On one hand, we had nothing to lose. It was fun, real, raw, we loved every minute of it, and we helped cool companies do amazing things. But on the other, our guts hurt from the punches. We bounced checks, slept at the office, experienced soul-crushing defeats, and Sunny got so thin from stress and anxiety that her family staged an intervention. Most of all, we were lonely.

While most of our friends were happily chipping away at college and waking up with shaving cream mustaches on their faces, we were slugging it out in boardrooms, getting schooled every which way, and growing up very, very fast.

To broaden our appeal, mentors and family members suggested we dial back our crazy ideas. Tame down the "fluffy" talk of vision and purpose. Take whatever work we could get our hands on. Don't ruffle feathers or have such strong opinions. Be like everybody else.

You have *no idea* how close we came.

After a few years of this, we started to cave. The relentless uphill struggle against a world that either didn't understand us or opposed us had turned our passion into dust. On a long drive, back from a pitch event we first bombed at (but ended up winning), the truth came out: Maybe we weren't cut out for entrepreneurship. Maybe our dreams were just . . . dreams. We got so discouraged that we thought about closing up shop. Why was this *so hard*? Why was everything such a dogfight? We felt like no one believed in us, and we were beginning to question whether we believed in ourselves.

After admitting life had kicked out every ounce of heart left for the business, we had a conversation with Sunny's dad, one of our greatest mentors. He warned us: "You two are a rare breed. Not everyone will love you. Some may hate you. But the ones who get you will never forget you. Now, dust yourselves off and get back in that saddle."

That message changed everything. *Of course* people didn't get us. We were doing things differently—breaking rules and vandalizing traditions. This was our identity, and we needed to own it. Instantly, we became more confident in tearing up the rule book, running our business on our own terms, and being who we were—not who we were *supposed* to be.

Instead of doing everything people told us we should be doing—be transactional, be conservative, be *agreeable*—we did the opposite. Instead of burying vices like our obsessive perfectionism, rebelliousness, and weirdness, we made them our *selling points*. What's more, the qualities that made us *us* also helped us connect powerfully with our clients, and within a few months, Motto began attracting global clients and scrappy startups that wanted to flip the script, too.

We might not have had a long pedigree in the branding industry or an iconic founder whose fifty-year-old principles we were supposed to follow, but we were cutting our teeth on the streets. Other agencies focused on niches and specializations. We focused on diversification, working across categories, verticals, industries, and trades. One minute we'd be branding a small startup, and the next, a two-billion-dollar giant. In doing so, we exposed ourselves to the inner workings, mindsets, and behaviors of a vast array of leaders and companies—the good, the bad, and the *surprising*.

We turned our attention not just to branding, but to leadership and identified a connection between the spirit of the person at the helm of a company and the brand experience that company created for its customers. The virtues (or vices) of that person inevitably made the company thrive, turn sideways, or fall apart.

This fascination with leadership quickly became the linchpin of our branding business. We became experts at helping leaders harness their superpowers, turning their businesses and brands into the "rare breed," or standout, in their category.

That shift in our thinking—in what we believed were our strengths—was the salvation of our company and the beginning of the concept of Rare Breed—the idea that the things that make us different, that other people consider to be weaknesses or vices, can in fact be the sources of our greatest strengths.

This new perspective changed more than just our company. When we stopped worrying about being "good enough," we were able to focus on nurturing and growing the parts of ourselves that made us great. Yes, we learned to *leverage* our innate qualities as strengths, but we also learned to *love* them. And in the end, we became more confident in other areas of our lives, not just the part that took place in our offices.

Our point of view proved wildly successful, eventually taking our agency from the Low Country of South Carolina to Dallas to New York City, from working with local rule-breakers to designing brands for the future of food, technology, retail, fashion, beauty, and humankind. Our clients include ambitious startups and household names like 20th Century Fox, *USA Today,* E. & J. Gallo Winery, and Legendary Digital Networks. Our work can be seen in Best Buy, Walmart, Starbucks, Target, CVS, Walgreens, Whole Foods, Costco, and hundreds more.

We now conduct workshops and consult with business leaders, teams, and organizations around the world on how to stand out using the Rare Breed mindset and virtues.

In the pages that follow, we'll share the lessons we've learned and the unconventional traits we've seen that can lead to great success. The traits we discovered aren't vices or things to fear—they are your greatest assets in becoming the creative, the leader, the human being you want to be. Although society often forces us to conform our "undesirable" qualities, we'll show you how to harness them, priming you to live and lead in ways you never thought possible.

Know this: you are not average. You already have what it takes to succeed and stand out. We're going to show that there are as many ways to *be* a Rare Breed as there are people who know they have more to give to the world. We hope this book will show you the way.

RARE BREED

INTRODUCTION

If You Want to Succeed, You Have to Own Who You Are

> In a society that profits from your self doubt, liking yourself is a rebellious act.
>
> —Caroline Caldwell

Maybe you're nineteen and wondering whether college is for you. Or thirty-seven and worried you'll have to ditch your startup dreams and get a real job. Or somewhere in between. It doesn't matter. You're probably like us when we started Motto. You're chasing an unruly vision, and you want success without compromising who you are, even if it means sacrifice and hardship.

Twentieth-century Trappist monk Thomas Merton captured that drive when he wrote, "If you want to identify me, ask not where I live, or what I like to eat, or how I comb my hair, but ask me what I think I am living for, in detail, and ask me what I think is keeping me from living fully for the thing I want to live for."

However, at the heart of thousands of business, leadership, and success books is a common theme: *success is conditional.* You can have a successful career, thriving business, and fulfilling life, but only if you work your way up the invisible ladder, grind down your prickly points, and march in time like a dutiful soldier, so you will, in that awful phrase, "fit in."

You've heard the whispers since middle school, like lines from a script you didn't write: *Don't create a ruckus. Keep your head down. Stop being so weird. Forget that crazy dream. Play it safe.*

Hidden among the systems and steps is a subtle and sinister message: You need to change who are you to succeed. There's something about you that's *flawed.*

A lot of people believe that. For them, playing safe, smoothing down rough edges, and "fitting in" works. It helps them find their success story by following the traditional blueprint: take classes, get the degree, and rise up one résumé-building promotion at a time.

However, that's not you. If you follow that traditional path, you risk becoming one of the people Martha Medeiros had in mind when she wrote: "He or she who does not turn things topsy-turvy, who is unhappy at work, who does not risk certainty for uncertainty, to thus follow a dream, those who do not forego sound advice at least once in their lives, dies slowly."

You prefer Henry David Thoreau: "I wanted to live deep and suck out all the marrow of life, to live so sturdily and Spartan-like as to put to rout all that was not life, to cut a broad swath and shave close, to drive life into a corner, and reduce it to its lowest terms."

Nobody ever called you compliant or predictable. There's a disorderly, independent, rogue, magnificent side to you that's unlike anyone else. You're like rapper Shawn Carter, who in 1994 couldn't get a record label to give him a deal. Instead of throwing in the towel, he founded his own record company and later changed his name to Jay-Z. What if, like him, you could take the parts of yourself other people criticize and turn them into superpowers? What if you could change your future not by becoming someone else, but by going all-in on who you are?

You can. We're going to show you how.

› Discovering the Rare Breed

In fifteen years at Motto, we've helped hundreds of leaders unlock their potential by tapping in to what makes them unique. In doing so, we found many of them to be obstinate, temperamental, melodramatic, and ruthless. For these swashbuckling visionaries, believing "six impossible things before breakfast" wasn't just a line from *Through the Looking-Glass*, it was a *business plan*—hell, a *life* plan. After a while, we realized that not only were the difficult ones more interesting to work with, but they also tended to be fearless entrepreneurs who inspired us with the audacity of their ideas and the intensity of their passions.

It hit us like a lightning bolt:

Being defiant, dangerous, and different is a gift.

That epiphany was a game changer. Success is no longer the purview of the Harvard MBA graduate. You don't need degrees or titles or venture capital. You just *decide* and *act*, and you can change the world because of it. Whether you're building eye-popping innovations with Kickstarter cash, filming award-winning documentaries with your iPhone, or launching social movements on Instagram, you don't need permission to lead or succeed. You can change the conversation not by *suppressing* your vices, but by *owning* them. Being a leader no longer means getting someone's seal of approval or following an accepted glide path. It means going all-in on who you are, grabbing the mantle of your career, and saying, "I got this." No apologies. No excuses.

In other words:

> Succeed not *despite* who you are, but *because* of who you are.

People like that . . . are what we call the Rare Breed.

Rare Breeds have always been with us. Joan of Arc was a Rare Breed. Mozart was a Rare Breed. Orson Welles was a Rare Breed. Lenny Bruce was a Rare Breed. Maya Angelou was one, too. These people unsentimentally tore down the conventions of their chosen fields and transformed them with their talent and vision.

Now, Rare Breeds include Tomi Adeyemi, the twenty-five-year-old author of the bestselling fantasy *Children of Blood and Bone*, who has shown young writers of color that there's a place for them in the lily-white world of swords and sorcery. You can count Malala Yousafzai, the Pakistani activist and winner of the Nobel Peace Prize who didn't let a round of bullets shoot down her vision of a world where all girls can learn and lead, among their ranks, too.

Rare Breeds live to their own beat and are indistinguishable from their calling. To get what they want—to realize visions that seem outlandish to the rest of the world—they sacrifice everything and stop at nothing. They are rebellious thinkers, relentless perfectionists, strange weirdoes, and spellbinding orators. They squeeze every ounce of talent from themselves and everybody around them. Until, one day, their potential is realized, and they change the world.

› Virtues, Mantras, and Stories

At the heart of this book are seven "vices"—seven traits that conventional wisdom regards as dangerous and counterintuitive to your success—that we've called Virtues. They are the keys to becoming a Rare Breed:

1. **REBELLIOUS.** Rare Breeds hurl themselves against the walls of business-as-usual to see what breaks.
2. **AUDACIOUS.** Rare Breeds see realities other people can't see and have the nerve to try to bring them into being, even when everyone else says they are impossible.
3. **OBSESSED.** Perfectionism isn't a bug for Rare Breeds; it's their operating system. They're all-in, always on, 24/7. Sketching at breakfast, practicing pitch lines in the shower, waking up with insane ideas at 4 a.m.
4. **HOT-BLOODED.** Rare Breeds come to the table with fire and fury that put others to shame.
5. **WEIRD.** Rare Breeds are *strange*. Know who else is strange? Astronauts. Poets. Nobel laureates. Artists. Inventors. Everyone who dares to do what makes us laugh, cry, swoon, or gasp in awe.
6. **HYPNOTIC.** Rare Breeds are spell-binding orators and seducers, conductors capable of leading the orchestra of people around them and inspiring others to fulfill their potential.
7. **EMOTIONAL.** Rare Breeds feel things deeply and trust their guts. They channel their emotions and show up with empathy, kindness, and intuition.

Each Virtue leads into a series of Mantras—unique stories of Rare Breeds, combined with unorthodox wisdom and practical tools we've learned along the way. Use them as guiding principles to build your career, business, or brand. Through these stories, you'll meet extraordinary Rare Breeds like actress and producer Lena Dunham, Supreme Court justice Ruth Bader Ginsburg, chefs Chad Houser and Daniel Boulud, sushi master Jiro Ono, advertising provocateur Cindy Gallop, inventor Sir James Dyson, legendary Swiss watchmaker Philippe Dufour, tennis star Serena Williams, music phenomenon Beyoncé, filmmaker Tim Burton, graffiti artist Banksy, and many, many more. They embody everything Rare Breeds are capable of.

› A Dangerous Duality

Of course, nothing good comes without risk, and each of the Virtues also has a seductive side, a dangerous duality you must pay attention to. What's more, the borderland between the light and dark sides of our nature is murky and indistinct, making it hard to tell which is which. As Carl Jung wrote, "There is no energy unless there is a tension of opposites; hence it is necessary to discover the opposite to the attitude of the conscious mind."

The film *Black Swan* neatly illustrates this perilous state. Natalie Portman's Nina begins as a creature of light, but the darker, more sinister side of her persona slowly becomes part of her everyday reality. Eventually, when she looks in the mirror, she sees not herself but her doppelgänger—the unrestrained, chaotic destroyer who descends into violence and madness.

For Rare Breeds, the impulses that uplift can also undo. Set loose without morality or control, hot-blooded passion can lead to rage and reckless, destructive acts. Charisma can spiral into a force that manipulates and defrauds. Obsessive perfectionism can lead to compulsive behaviors, endless work, burnout, and alienation. Rebels can lose sight of their cause and go on a rampage for the sake of sheer destruction.

As you'll see through the people whose stories we tell, from Avicii to Icarus, the hazards of this duality are very real. We'll confront them, discuss them, and look at ways we can prevent them from sabotaging us.

› What We Hope You'll Take Away

You might be wondering: Can I be a Rare Breed?

The answer is an emphatic "*maybe*." Rare Breeds are, in fact, rare. What separates Rare Breeds from everyone else is one simple truth: while others may suppress their quirky, oddball, pain-in-the-ass qualities, Rare Breeds *lean in* to theirs. They celebrate them and let them off the leash, break the windows of conventional wisdom, and run like hooligans through the corridors of entrenched power.

In a world that wants to own you, owning yourself in this way can hurt like hell. The Rare Breed life is not one of least resistance; it's *hard*. And not everyone is cut out for it.

If you're reading this, you may be young and eager, ready to shake things up and put the world on notice. Or you may be enjoying some success and wondering what's next. Maybe you're smarting from a failure and trying to figure out how to stage your comeback. Or you may be an experienced leader or executive feeling like you've hit a wall and asking, "What more can I do?"

No matter where you're at, we hope you'll use *Rare Breed* as a guide for understanding, unlocking, and directing the potential that's been slumbering in you. The secret to doing that? Own it. Learn to accept and love yourself for who you are: worthy and valuable, "vices" (Virtues!) and all. Don't just march to the beat of your own drum; build your own drums out of wire, garbage, and spare parts.

Some readers will disagree with the premise of *Rare Breed*. Maybe they want more generic advice, or more scientific evidence. They'll pick up the book in the airport bookstore, read the jacket, snarl "What's this nonsense?," and toss it back on the shelf. Others won't like it because we talk about provocative topics, politicians, social issues, sex, gender, religion, and more. They'll snap, "Stay in your lane!"

Fuck the lane.

We didn't write this book for those people. We wrote it for you—for anyone who feels like they don't fit in. For anyone who wants to lead, create, inspire, and provoke change on their own terms by harnessing *all* of who they are, not just the pretty parts. It's a new conversation for a new era.

Let's begin.

VIRTUE 1

REBELLIOUS

Defiant. Disruptive. Ungovernable. Rogue. Insubordinate.

An asset when your rebellious spirit is harnessed to push boundaries, confront wrongs, give a voice to the voiceless, or birth something unprecedented.

A weakness when expressed with malice or bitterness, or for no reason other than to stir up trouble, create unnecessary chaos, or get revenge.

Andrew Jackson stares out at you from the $20 bill like he's daring you to kick up some shit. He looks every inch the warrior nicknamed "Old Hickory." What kind of person does it take to give one of history's most controversial presidents the heave-ho from his place of honor? Try an even bigger badass named Harriet Tubman. There are plans to have her replace Jackson on the twenty in the coming years.

Tubman was the real deal. Born a slave in the early 1820s, she once said, "There was one of two things I had a right to, liberty or death; if I could not have one, I would have the other." It's hard to imagine a more courageous, hazardous way of rebelling against the system than escaping from slavery not once but *twice* in 1849, but that's what Tubman did, following the legendary Underground Railroad north to Pennsylvania and on to freedom.

The Fugitive Slave Act of 1850 dictated that all escaped slaves had to be returned to their masters upon capture, even if they were in free states. So it would have been understandable if Tubman had chosen to keep her head down in the North, stay quiet, adopt a new identity, and avoid unnecessary risk. Maybe join a book club and take up needlepoint? We weren't there, but we're pretty sure her response to the idea would've been, "Fuck that."

But instead, she headed to Maryland many more times, helping fifty or sixty family and friends move North and earning the nickname "Moses." Retirement time, right? Hardly. Once the Civil War began, Tubman was part of a military expedition that liberated hundreds of slaves in South Carolina. She also worked as a cook, a nurse, and a spy during the Civil War and later foreshadowed Rosa Parks's activism by refusing to move into the smoking car of a train.

For Tubman, rebelling was an asset: she used it to transform her oppression and frustration into action and did something no one had done before on such a grand scale. That rebellious Rare Breed spirit could have sabotaged her efforts, but instead, she used this inherent part of herself as a strength. About her efforts, she said, "I can't die but once." That's not just a rebel talking. That's a bona fide hero.

> I had crossed the line. I was free; but there was no one to welcome me to the land of freedom. I was a stranger in a strange land; and my home, after all, was down in Maryland, because my father, my mother, my brothers, and sister, and friends were there. But I was free, and they should be free.
>
> **—Harriet Tubman to Sarah Bradford,**
> ***Scenes in the Life of Harriet Tubman*, 1868**

› You've Been Conditioned

If rebels are such a powerful force, why don't more people head for the horizon, defy conventional wisdom, or refuse to conform? From where we sit, it looks like a lot of people are waiting for permission. If that's you, you could be waiting a *long* time.

We've been conditioned to believe that rebels are troublemakers, renegades, and law-breakers. The connotations of the word can be misleading: The word *rebel* suggests leather-jacketed teens with bad attitudes, tatted-up punk rockers, and other mischievous outsiders. We think of them as people who break the rules for the hell of it and create unnecessary conflict. They're the ones with hooks for hands and scars on their faces who lie, cheat, and steal: Jesse James, who robbed banks and trains; Billy the Kid, who is said to have killed eight men before he was himself gunned down at age twenty-one.

But not all rebels are like that: Frederick Douglass was a rebel. Eve was a rebel when she took the first bite of that forbidden apple.

When you get right down to it, all *rebel* really means is somebody who does what society has deemed unacceptable or abnormal, or that others fear or don't understand. More often than not, history has ultimately shown that the problem rests with the conventional thinking, *not* with those who disobey or transform it. In fact, most of the advancements we've seen in all areas of human life—from business to art to science to politics—have occurred because of rebels.

Still, the fear of rebels shapes our modern mindset. It penetrates our parenting, careers, leadership, and companies. Snuck out at midnight? *You're grounded.* Made a ruckus in class? *Off to the principal's office.* Broke a dumb rule at work? *You're fired.* We're taught to obey authority figures and not question the way things are done. That's why so many of us grow into repressed adults, our rebellious spirit like an animal in a cage caterwauling to be turned loose. We spend our lives obeying someone else's voice instead of listening to our own.

Here's what's interesting: all those other voices telling us what to do aren't just noise. They influence how we behave. In *Origins of Madness: Psychopathology in Animal Life* (1979), J. D. Keehn describes how laboratory animals are conditioned to accept that being part of experiments is simply part of their daily existence:

> As the animal enters the laboratory room and takes its station in the restraining harness, its habitual self-imposed restraint forces it to submit to the "rules and regulations" of the testing hour. The animal does not rebel against these familiar rules and regulations because, through training, it has relinquished its freedom of action and, for the hour, becomes a passive agent responding to the experimenters' signals as best it can.

Just like that, forced repetition teaches an animal to accept completely unnatural conditions that would normally have it spitting and clawing for its life.

Given enough time and pressure, humans become just as docile. We play nice. We don't question. We limit ourselves. We follow the rules that society determines are necessary for order and control. But that's not the kind of life any of us is meant to live.

In the 2011 documentary *Steve Jobs: One Last Thing*, Jobs comments on the power inherent in refusing to accept a small, limited life:

> When you grow up, you tend to get told that the world is the way it is and your life is just to live your life inside the world—try not to bash into the walls too much, try to have a nice family life, have fun, save a little money. That's a very limited life. Life can be much broader once you discover one simple fact: everything around you that you call life was made up by people that were no smarter than you. And you can change it, you can influence it, you can build your own things . . . Once you learn that, you'll never be the same again.

Fist bump, Steve.

› Rebels Move the World Forward

Harriet Tubman would have understood exactly what Jobs was talking about, and we rebellious Rare Breeds are all her spiritual heirs. If you've ever had the urge to step out of line, stand on your desk, and tell The Man "Enough!," you're part of the Rebel Alliance. You can pick up your insignia in the room down the hall.

Rebellion is evolution, the overthrow of the good for the better. The status quo gives ground grudgingly, so rebels are *needed* to challenge corrupt regimes and social codes, dethrone outdated systems, and force us all, sometimes kicking and screaming, into the future.

Case in point: Emma González, the seventeen-year-old from Marjory Stoneman Douglas High School who stood fiercely at a podium in Fort Lauderdale, Florida, to give legislators and the National Rifle Association a piece of her mind after her classmates had been gunned down. She repeated common tropes used to undermine gun control laws, and after each, stated, "We call BS."

Our most pivotal moments are about rebels who look at a reality that is intolerable (and that everyone assumes can't be challenged) and say, "I won't stand for another minute of this!"

From the Founding Fathers flipping a "We hold these truths to be self-evident" bird to the British Empire to Elvis in the 1950s whose performances were so charged with pelvis thrusting that panicked newspapers ran headlines like "Beware of Elvis Presley!," rebellion breeds legends who have historic effect. Rare Breed rebels are often considered outrageous at the time, until their radical natures are recognized as tools for change and societal development. We admire and revere those who risk everything to stand up for what they believe is right. Even if we don't agree with their cause, we love that they fight for it.

That's why rebellious is our prime Virtue, the headwaters of this raging Rare Breed river. Everything else we'll talk about Rare Breeds doing—following an audacious vision, turning obsessive perfectionism into world-class excellence, fueling the fire in their bellies—starts when the conformist says, "You'll never crack the human genome," and the rebel says, "Really? Hold my drink."

Saying that is more possible today than at any time in history. Rebellion has gone from being a once-in-a-lifetime thing to part of our cultural DNA. In business, rebellions happen daily. Industries are built on overthrowing what's gone before. Technology has made it easier, but it's our mindset—the idea that not only *can* we break free and chart our own course, but that we're *supposed* to—that gets most of the credit. Today, anyone can bring about radical change.

> Disobedience, in the eyes of anyone who has read history, is man's original virtue. It is through disobedience that progress has been made, through disobedience and rebellion.
>
> —Oscar Wilde, "The Soul of Man Under Socialism," 1891

› Take Up Arms Against Conformity

When author and researcher Francesca Gino surveyed more than one thousand employees in a range of industries, fewer than 10 percent said they worked in companies that regularly encouraged nonconformity. As she wrote in the *Harvard Business Review*, they "urge employees to check a good chunk of their real selves at the door."

If you're stuck in a broken organization that doesn't give a damn about your renegade thinking, you're not alone. Most organizations fear the rebel. We bet you know what it's like to be trapped in that sort of conformist machine. You feel smothered and bored. You're sick of proposing daring, brave ideas and getting a rebuke instead of a reward. As you watch *other* people do the challenging, career-making work you should be doing, jealousy kicks in.

But you're not under anybody's thumb. You're naturally driven to push limits, to challenge taboos, to disrupt and confound. You relish the idea of striking terror in the hearts of powerful, comfortable people. Contrariness is your modus operandi. Complacency is your eighth deadly sin. Your spirit animal is two raised arms with middle fingers extended.

Deep down, you've always been that pugnacious punk with your chin in the air—the skeptic, the infidel, the kid who points out that the emperor has no clothes. But for as long as you can remember, you've felt like the only person who saw the hypocrisy in the system, the only one asking, "It's obvious to you how they're manipulating us, right? RIGHT?"

Now you're ready to right injustices or to show the world how to do something smarter, greener, or more humane. You have a secret notebook bursting with rebellious ideas that will flip corporations on their heads, product designs that will change how the world works, or political messages that actually *mean* something. They tick away in your mind like explosive devices, waiting for you to push the detonator.

So why haven't you pushed it? Because fitting in is more comfortable than bucking convention. Psychological studies show that conformity isn't just a learned behavior in humans, it's innate. And so, faced with the consequences of deviating from social expectations, you find yourself wishing you could be content being comfortably numb, like the rest of the sheeple.

But you can't, because you're a rebel. So was Harriet Tubman. She didn't start out as a legend. At one point she was just a young woman looking down the barrel of a terrifying choice: spend life as a slave or abandon everything she'd ever known, risking capture, torture, and death to find freedom. She's a Rare Breed because she found the courage to make that choice.

Here's your chance to stir up the rebellious Rare Breed within you. Rebels are ordinary people who do extraordinary things. You're no different from them, because being a rebel isn't about *not* being scared. It's about feeling the anxiety and pushing the button anyway.

If you're willing to walk away from what you know to create something new, you're a rebel. If you're willing to step out of your comfort zone to right a wrong, you're a rebel. If you speak up when nobody else does, you're a rebel. And if you're a rebel, you're a leader, too.

> Recall how often in human history the saint and the rebel have been the same person.
>
> —**Rollo May, *The Courage to Create***

> The Dark Side of Rebellious

Used with respect and restraint, rebelliousness is a force of nature, a controlled burn that clears land for new growth. But tearing things down out of sheer malice can end up setting a wildfire that can and might easily destroy everything you've worked for.

Look at the most infamous rebel of all time: Satan. In Milton's *Paradise Lost*, he's unwilling to live under what he sees as God's tyranny, so he rebels, and he and his army is cast into Hell, where he says:

> . . . Here at least
> We shall be free; th' Almighty hath not built
> Here for his envy, will not drive us hence:
> Here we may reign secure, and in my choyce
> To reign is worth ambition though in Hell:
> Better to reign in Hell, than serve in Heav'n.

Really? We're willing to bet Hell wasn't Plan A.

The thing that separates the heroic rebel from the nihilistic agent of chaos is *service*. Who or what is your rebellion serving? Take one of the most famous rebels of literature, Robin Hood. Seeing his people taxed into poverty and brutalized in the absence of the king, he and his band of merry misfits rebelled against abusive authority to bring justice to the powerless. Robin wasn't serving himself; he was rebelling to right a wrong and protect others. That's noble.

One of the most infamous real-life rebels of the twentieth century, Adolf Hitler, had no such moral compass. He was a rebel—of the worst kind. He used his power to bend Germany to his will, killing millions and igniting the Second World War. His only concern was making himself ever more powerful.

Rebellions throw off destruction like a fire gives off smoke, and destruction can be addictive. Just ask the arsonist standing outside a burning building, face upturned to the flames in pure ecstasy. If your act of rebellion isn't serving something greater than yourself, you can become an avatar of anarchy. If you're a rebel willing to walk a solitary path for the good of other people, you can become a Rare Breed.

> Mildred: Hey, Johnny, what are you rebelling against?
> Johnny: Whaddya got?
>
> —*The Wild One*, 1953

› Putting Rebellious to Work

Whether you're building your career or a business of your own, you have a big advantage: *Nobody ever sees the rebel coming.* The established players in any industry are always fat, sluggish, and content. You're defiant, swift, and hungry. Because your ideas are daring (and probably defiant), you'll blindside the competition. By the time they catch on, you've picked their pockets, stolen their best customers, and won the admiring press.

As a rebel, you *will* meet resistance, but you look forward to it. Rebellion is an act of war. The established order always counterpunches and usually wears brass knuckles. As you're getting ready to make your move, ask four important questions:

1. WHAT AM I REBELLING AGAINST?

In a rebellion, your adversary defines you. Without that iceberg, the *Titanic* was just another ship. Without Sauron, Gandalf is just a hippie in a robe. If you don't know what (or who) you're fighting, you could find yourself punching air. Is it another company? A social code? The practices of an industry? A political ideology? Be crystal clear about your adversary, get to know it well, then play off its weaknesses.

2. WHAT NEEDS TO CHANGE?

Know exactly how you want to disrupt the status quo. You can't improvise a mission; you have to have an idea not only of what you want to tear down, but what you hope to build in its place. The cost of rebellion is high; without a cause, you or the people who follow you won't keep paying it.

3. WHAT DO I HAVE THAT NOBODY ELSE HAS?

What's your selling point or contentious point of view? Why should someone believe in you or follow you? Can you double down on your roguish personality and devil-may-care wit? You'll need to show up knowing exactly what makes you like nobody else. If you're not sure what makes you special, start by jumping on social media and asking, "In one or two sentences, how would you describe me? What makes me interesting to you?" You'll be surprised how many people will help you look in the mirror.

4. WHAT'S THE WORST THAT COULD HAPPEN?

Fear of the unknown is always worse than the actual unknown. What's the worst that could happen if you rebel against everything you know to chase your vision? You get your ass handed to you, sure. So what? You get some great stories, learn some lessons, build partnerships, and discover that defeat and death aren't the same thing. What's the worst that could happen if you *don't* rebel? You stagnate. You regret. You spend your life asking, "What if?"

The following Mantras are your guide to kicking up the rebellious Rare Breed within. In each of these stories someone chose to take a stand, face the headwinds, and keep going. Here's to getting in some good, necessary trouble.

1

FUCK NORMS

Norms begin as behaviors or social codes that make the majority of people feel safe and operate at ease. Given enough time to sit unchallenged, norms harden like petrified wood and turn into rigid beliefs: "This is the way things are done." Most people don't question them; the few who do are punished. Without norms that tell us what we should or shouldn't do, our world would be in chaos, and we wouldn't know how to navigate it.

Or so we're told.

In *The Rules of Sociological Method* (1895), the French sociologist Émile Durkheim defined the term "social fact"—that is, things such as institutions, values, and beliefs that exist outside the individual and can constrain those who don't think or act as they dictate. Those who feel oppressed by such social facts, or norms, are given two options: surrender or exile. But there's a third, rebellious option: fuck the norm.

Fucking norms is a powerful strategy for gaining an advantage, because when broken, they often bring about a knee-jerk reaction. Most people are shocked, perplexed, and fascinated despite themselves, staring at you slack-jawed, saying, "How in hell did you *do* that?" Sure, the guardians of propriety usually respond with everything from shame campaigns to lawsuits. But amid the blowback, you'll find a dissatisfied minority dying for someone to rattle society's cage and give them another option.

› Fuck Gender Norms: The Story of Wildfang

Emma Mcilroy and Julia Parsley had a secret that turned out to be a secret *power.* The two former Nike execs, although model employees, weren't Nike customers. They weren't anybody's customer, really. Because they liked dressing, to put it in conventional terms, like men. On weekends, they'd hit up stores like Urban Outfitters and slip over to the men's section to find sartorial treasures like fedoras, blazers, and graphic tees.

It kind of sucked though. The clothes didn't fit right, and Mcilroy and Parsley had to crash the party of another gender to get the look they wanted. They tried other ways too, like consulting Google for "tomboy fashion," but the only result was "Where can I find tomboy fashion?" A series of connections happened, one after the other, like toppling dominos. *There must be a lot of other women like us out there who want to dress the same way we do,* they thought. A memory resurfaced: Parsley recalled that her grandmother told her that in the 1950s, she improvised the wardrobe she had wanted by raiding her husband's closet. The unspoken need had existed for *decades,* and yet nobody had keyed in to it or had the guts to act on it in a large-scale way.

Who knows how many women were, or had been, at the same crossroads as Mcilroy and Parsley? Or how many women even *recognized* the moment as a crossroads at all? So, during an afternoon of shopping in 2010, they asked themselves not *What if there were a store for women like us?* but the more revolutionary question, *Why don't we CREATE a store for women like us?*

And just like that, Wildfang was born.

It wasn't easy: For fifteen months, they lived off their 401(k) savings and worked out of an apartment. They did this armed with nothing but an idea, the passion to pursue it, and the confidence that it would work. And this, too, is part and parcel of being a Rare Breed.

When they launched with just a landing page, before they even had a product line, twenty-two thousand women signed up for their email list in just one month. When their product debuted, it found an immediate audience, including Hollywood tomboys Kate Moennig, Ellen Page, Kate Mara, and Evan Rachel Wood.

Mcilroy and Parsley were uniquely qualified to recognize that their observation was loaded with opportunity. We think of it as "striking oil"—that moment when a gusher erupts, releasing something powerful that's been pent up just under the surface, and also has great value.

From their bendingly cool name, implying something animal, powerful, and a little dangerous; to their whole team, who go about their work knowing what a difference it makes in people's lives; to their message, which screams "Fuck Norms!"—they have a voice that comes through loud, clear, and unapologetic.

The core idea of Wildfang is breathtakingly simple: it steals styles from guys and fits them for women. The company inspires women to wear whatever the hell they want and spares them the awkwardness and stigma of ever having to set foot in the men's department again.

We're crushing on this company's manifesto so hard we're thinking of asking it to prom:

> Wildfang is not a brand. We are a band. More specifically, we are a band of thieves. Modern-day, female Robin Hoods raiding men's closets and maniacally dispensing blazers, cardigans, wingtips, and bowlers as we roam from town to town in these stolen styles of ours. . . . We're here to liberate menswear one bowtie at a time and we're doing it ourselves because we want it done right.

Mic *sooo* dropped.

There's also a wonderful sense that in realizing their vision for Wildfang, these two women realized a vision of *themselves*. The fact that they have inspired so many others makes a huge point: they tapped in to something that was already there but that others hadn't had the vision to recognize or the guts to pursue. Wildfang's customers didn't start dressing the way they do because of the company; the company made it easier and safer for them to express themselves the way they always wanted to. To be their true selves. To know that they were part of something bigger.

Think about it for a moment and you realize that when people say "Fuck norms," they don't mean any harm or hostility; all they mean is that *they* want to be free of the norms that have been imposed on them and others like them for generations.

› How to Own This Mantra

Fucking norms is a power move. Start by questioning dominant paradigms—how we grow our food, how we teach our children, how we make career decisions. Mcilroy and Parsley questioned why men's fashion could be worn only by men—something personally meaningful to them—and came up with their own answer.

Which norms restrict what you can do and who you can be? Why are you following them? If you disobeyed the rules, what could you build? Most important, would breaking those rules open a world of new opportunities, and would that world be worth the blowback?

Start to see things for what they really are: constructs—like the arena from the *Hunger Games*. It looks real, but shoot an arrow at it and you'll see that there's a manufactured, illusory boundary around the whole thing.

Look at how other work environments, families, cultures, or communities do things. What rules or codes restrict *them* from thriving? Locate populations isolated by age, gender, race, class, faith, orientation, disability, or injustice. What are the norms that confine them but make no sense?

You'll begin to notice patterns, the zero-substance regulations on how to think or act that are there only *because that's the way it is.* What transformative experiences are people missing out on because your industry has settled on one model and said, "That'll do"?

The most important question to ask is, of course, "What if?"

- ➔ What if we could 3D-print houses for the homeless? (ICON)
- ➔ What if we brought ethical factories and radical transparency to the fashion industry? (Everlane)
- ➔ What if we could democratize beauty? (Fenty Beauty by Rihanna)
- ➔ What if we turned ugly produce and scrap waste into delicious cold-pressed juice? (Misfit Foods)

When you've banked some knowledge, look for a way to redefine the rules. When you're ready for the big reveal, share what you're doing with everyone like it's your personal vendetta. Project your new rip-roaring documentary film on the side of a building during First Friday. Debut your clever design for a low-cost portable bicycle by staging a 10K fun ride. Graffiti your brand on sidewalks at 3 a.m.

Most important, launch like a rocket—loud and startling. That will leave you with no way back in case you start to lose your nerve. You've got this. Remember, norms can look cozy and comforting . . . but so can a casket.

2

VIOLATE ETIQUETTE

We must stop being polite and behaved and find new inventive tactics to shift the paradigm.

—Eve Ensler, "One Billion Rising"

Manners are a lubricant that allow people to rub together without friction. We are often taught through our experiences that, above everything else, we should be polite. No matter what we want to say or how we feel, the expected response to being uncomfortable or offended by someone or something is to just sit there, smile, and nod. Politeness is designed to keep things respectful. But what if what's being said or done is disrespectful?

Not everything *deserves* politeness, or civility. There are times when you need to stop playing nice and start raising hell.

Don't get us wrong, *Please* and *Thank You* should not disappear from your vocabulary. You need to be a good human and treat people right. Open doors for others. Say "hi" to strangers. But etiquette for etiquette's sake can lead to sacrificing your own feelings and beliefs for the comfort of others. There's a fine line between being well-behaved and being compliant. Rebellious Rare Breeds stride across that line, erasing it as they go. They violate etiquette because they know this:

The person who misbehaves has the floor.

Lena Dunham, the writer/comedian/actress/provocateur who created the groundbreaking HBO show *Girls*, is also the first woman to win, in 2013, a Directors Guild of America Award for Outstanding Directing—Comedy Series. She's made *Time*'s list of the one hundred most influential people in the world and is a bestselling author whose 2014 book *Not That Kind of Girl: A Young Woman Tells You What She's "Learned"* was a publishing sensation.

But Dunham is also another kind of threat: she's a threat to the status quo, a disruptive force ready to take on the closed-minded at every turn. If you look deeper into the source of her fame and the nature of it, you'll realize that everything she's become began with challenging an unspoken code of etiquette.

With *Girls*, Dunham rejected the standard ladylike, cool-girl-living-in-New-York trope you've see on classic, female-led shows like *Sex and the City* and instead took viewers into an uncensored, un-gussied-up girl's-eye view of the world. She and her friends weren't breezing off to martini lunches and living in Manhattan flats that only a Hilton heiress could afford. They were blundering, scared, real women trying to get through life without screwing things up too badly.

But one of the most defining aspects of the show, and of Dunham's etiquette-defying attitude, was that she constantly showed off her very average, imperfect naked body to the world. That violated a major unspoken entertainment commandment: *Thou shalt not depict any nude female body onscreen that is not sleek and flawless.* Dunham's body was neither, and her actions forced viewers to confront their expectations of a female star and ask themselves what was more important for a strong performance: incredible talent or a tight ass?

Nobody likes being called out for their own douchey-ness, so Dunham caught bloody hell for it. But to her credit, she seemed to thrive on the controversy. She didn't ask permission. She didn't apologize. She simply did it, and forced us to admit that as a culture we still value women mostly for their beauty and sexuality. In the end, Dunham helped shift society's restricting ideas of the female body image and opened the door for a more diverse feminine identity that paved the way for other inclusive images of women like the TV show *Insecure* and the Indy movie *Patti Cake$*.

What takes Dunham's rebelliousness from mere bravery to something verging on heroic is that she tried something similar in her Oberlin College days. In a short film called *The Fountain*, she appeared brushing her teeth in a bikini. The film became a viral sensation on YouTube: many viewers were aghast at her un-shy displaying of her imperfect body; others defended her. "There were just pages of YouTube comments about how fat I was, or how not fat I was," Dunham said. "I didn't want you to Google me and the first thing you see is a debate about whether my breasts are misshapen."

When Dunham decided to go even further on *Girls*, she had to know from experience what to expect, and she surely anticipated that the response would be exponentially greater, thanks to her celebrity and the show's HBO platform. And yet, she did it anyway, and taught us all something: violating etiquette gives a person untold power to create real change and alter perceptions.

And that person can be *you*.

In a world where women are conditioned to be ashamed of just about everything—from enjoying sex to having a body that isn't model-perfect—Dunham's bold display of her sexuality, imperfection, and plain old lust for life forces haters to confront their own motivations.

More important, it gives women a role model of fearlessness. And it teaches us all that there's power in rebelliousness—and violating etiquette: Dunham's show ran for six seasons on HBO, her book sold for $3.5 million after furious bidding, and everybody waits with bated breath to see what she'll do next.

› How to Own This Mantra

To take up space in the world without apology, you might have to stop being polite and start getting real.

Recently, we were on a video call with a high-profile CEO and his marketing director. They were launching a new, innovative product and wanted us to brand it. The account was worth several hundred thousand dollars, so we were excited to see whether there was a fit.

As the marketing director began sharing the project details, things started getting *tense* between her and the CEO. Within minutes, the CEO was bullying and belittling her in a strange twist of power games. At one point, he even mimed a throat slash gesture while the poor lady was in mid-sentence, signaling her to shut up so that *he* could talk.

It was uncomfortable to watch. So, Ashleigh decided to end the meeting with a few direct words to the CEO: "I'm afraid we'll have to cut this short. The bulldozing of your colleague is unsettling."

Sure, we could've brushed it off or looked the other way. It would've been far easier to get through the call and say nothing, like we had done in the past—like we've *all* done. But it felt wrong.

Later that afternoon, we got an email from the marketing director who said she had put in her resignation and thanked us for speaking out on what had become a regular occurrence. She said, "Your courage showed me my own."

This taught us a valuable lesson. Many people tolerate, and even accept, all kinds of unacceptable behavior, because they feel they have no other choice. Actress Jennifer Lawrence, star of films like *American Hustle*, *Joy*, and *Red Sparrow*, revealed a "humiliating" and "degrading" incident that took place during her formative years in Hollywood. "A female producer had me do a nude lineup with about five women who were much, much thinner than me," Lawrence said. "We all stood side-by-side with only tape covering our privates," after which "the female producer told me I should use the naked photos of myself as inspiration for my diet." She went on to admit, "I let myself be treated a certain way because I felt I had to for my career."

If you find yourself exposed to the ugly, unspoken realities of your field that everyone wallpapers over with back slaps and smiling nods, then speak up. Are you witness to business models that screw over customers? Hidden racism? Technology with fatal flaws no one will cop to?

Refuse to politely look the other way. Be the one who calls out the corruption or injustice. Not with anger or spite, but in a direct, sincere way that changes the conversation for the better. When you hit a nerve, you'll have everyone's attention.

Call out rivals and their shady practices. Write about policies that need to be challenged. If accepted codes of conduct are standing in the way of your success or everybody's growth, contest them. Don't be afraid to put people in their place when they act inappropriately. That's how you violate etiquette.

That can be hard, especially when it's socially awkward, or you're dealing with someone who has authority over you, or your job is on the line. But you're not a doormat. Sunny's mom, Crystal, used to always tell us, "People treat you how you allow them to." Anytime anyone tries to make us feel less-than, we hear her voice saying those words, and we find our courage. The next time you are in a position with a put-down artist, or you're expected to bite your tongue and be proper as etiquette demands, remember that the most important person you should never violate is yourself.

3

NEVER PUNT

Swim upstream. Go the other way. Ignore the conventional wisdom.

—Sam Walton, *Sam Walton: Made in America*

Thousands of years ago conventional wisdom said that the earth was a pancake. That theory was proved wrong thanks to some brilliant scientists, philosophers, and mathematicians who eventually determined that the earth was, in fact, a sphere. That is, unless you're a conspiracy theorist and member of the Flat Earth Society, who after all these years, *still* can't accept the truth.

Conventional wisdom is defined as ideas so rigorously accepted that they go unquestioned. Many examples of when conventional wisdom led us astray are etched in the history books because of how blatantly wrong they were. Common knowledge can be deceptive because it gives us an excuse to stop questioning and accept that things are what they are. But what if the old ideas of what you know to be true aren't true at all?

This brings us to Kevin Kelley, a man who sees football differently from, well, *everyone*. He's the longstanding head coach and athletic director of Pulaski Academy in Little Rock, Arkansas, and he's achieved great success for the Bruins with a startling, counterintuitive approach to the game: his teams *never punt* the ball. Ever.

Most people would call Coach Kelley's defiance of one hundred years of traditional football wisdom crazy, but it's all based on a sophisticated statistical analysis of probability that he learned from a Harvard study. The report analyzed two thousand football games over three years and concluded that field position wasn't as important as most coaches believe. Kelley did the math on conversion probabilities and realized that if he didn't punt on the fourth down, his team would convert about 50 percent of its fourth-down plays to keep touchdown drives alive. Basically, *punting is stupid.*

Armed with mounds of mathematical data, a rabble-rousing spirit to tear up the playbook, and a drive to increase game wins, in 2008 Kelley started changing the way he ran his football team. His strange new strategy meant no more punting like every other football team. They started onside kicking after every score, and even incorporated rugby-style plays into the game. It was rogue and it worked. At the close of its 2018 season, Pulaski Academy's football team had a 179-25-1 record, with seven state championships under its belt.

Despite the success, Kelley has seen his fair share of eye rolling and criticism from other coaches who are wedded to convention and find comfort in losing traditionally over attempting to win radically. Copycats have yet to spring up at higher levels. "It all comes down to risk aversion," Kelley says. "A lot of the coaches I've talked to will say, 'We think you're right. We think our team should do it too.' But then they're afraid of the media attacks or the fans not being supportive or losing their jobs." Kelley is totally cool with being the lone wolf because if every team adopts no-punting, he loses the strategic advantage.

As the first coach to adopt a no-punt philosophy, Kelley has become a cult figure in the sports community and has been featured on numerous national media outlets. His never-punt strategy was also recognized by *Time* magazine as the thirty-third best invention of 2009. The beautiful thing is that truth is like a lion: once you set it free, it defends itself.

› How to Own This Mantra

If you're feeling frozen in place, like a prehistoric bug trapped in amber, it could be because you're accepting conventional wisdom. What kind of "wisdom" are we talking about?

- → You need a college degree to do that.
- → You have to climb the corporate ladder first.
- → Women/men don't do that job.
- → You're too young to know what you're doing.
- → You're too old to start.
- → You need the right background.
- → You must have a plan, or you'll fail.
- → You need more money to succeed.

Forget about what "everybody knows" is true, because much of the time, it's not. Ask yourself a few questions:

- → Am I unconsciously following precepts that just don't make sense?
- → What is limiting what I can accomplish?
- → How can I rethink the rules of the game in my field?
- → How could I build a brand, company, or team if there were no templates to follow?
- → How could I lead if no one was around to tell me how?

As a Rare Breed, you can't overthrow conventional wisdom by mindlessly parroting what holy writ tells you is right. And you're too savvy to throw out a method *just because.* Take smart, calculated risks that let you venture far into the unknown, where the gold is. Dig into the data, like Kevin Kelley did, and find out what's really going on.

When you hit the point where everyone else seems to accept something as a given, be the outlier who questions what no one else will. *Why* do we always punt the ball? *Why* shouldn't someone kneel during the national anthem? *Why* does a drug cost more in this country than that country?

Coach Kelley found that every coach he knew punted because that's what everybody else did. He had the good sense to ask why.

4

EXPECT SABOTAGE

Remember Isaac Newton's First Law from high school physics? Well, if you're science-challenged like Ashleigh and you erased that class from your memory, here's a refresher: objects at rest stay at rest, and objects in motion stay in motion, with the same speed and in the same direction, unless acted upon by an external force.

In other words, the status quo wants to stay the status quo.

So, it's perfectly reasonable to expect sabotage when you rub against the status quo. You know that challenging biases and preconceptions, even if those challenges cause tension, is *good* for us. That's how we make progress. You also know that when you stand out, you slap a big fat target on your back. You're outside of the routine experience, and that makes you a threat to small minds, fearful souls, your inner circle, and terrified competitors, who will try to sabotage you.

Like in 2014 when Uber tried to sabotage its main competitor, Lyft, by having 177 employees book and then cancel more than five thousand rides. Ahem, *allegedly.* Right-wing groups regularly send provocateurs to Black Lives Matter protests to incite violence and turn people against the movement. Political candidates even have a term—*opposition research*—for their attempts to smear and discredit their opponents. (Google "Steele dossier" if you want a taste.)

The more you do that threatens or tries to change the establishment, the more likely you are to be feared and attacked. Whatever you're up against isn't going to take it lying down.

› Chobani Fights for Refugees

The story of Hamdi Ulukaya is a story of American entrepreneurship. Born in a small Turkish town known for producing some of the best cheese in the country, Ulukaya emigrated from Turkey to the United States in 1994. In 2005 he purchased a defunct yogurt factory and began making his own yogurt, which he called Chobani. The product was a smash hit; sales reached more than $1 billion in just five years, and Chobani is now the number one yogurt brand in the United States.

However, Ulukaya views his role as CEO as more than turning profits. For a long time he has hired refugees and immigrants, and he advocates for other US businesses to do the same. This hiring practice has drawn the ire of conspiracy theorists and the alt-right, which have accused Ulukaya of importing Muslims into the country for nefarious purposes.

Let the sabotage begin.

Right-wing news sites called for a boycott of Chobani, and Ulukaya has even received death threats, as did the mayor of Twin Falls, Idaho, where the Chobani plant is located, for supporting him. But these perils haven't stopped this rebellious Rare Breed from continuing to lead while fighting to improve the lives of some of the world's 25.4 million refugees. He's fought back with lawsuits, and he even rewarded his employees in 2016 by giving them 10 percent of the company. He continues to brush aside his critics to pursue his mission, saying, "Fear does not make great yogurt."

› How to Own This Mantra

You've upset the equilibrium and created discomfort. Some people will react negatively to what you stand for and launch a campaign of sabotage to bring you down. That's the moment of truth. You might feel yourself waver and be tempted to step away from the edge. Don't.

Instead, do these things:

RECOGNIZE AN ACT OF SABOTAGE FOR WHAT IT REALLY IS—an insecure reaction to a shift in power. Saboteurs are trying to cling to whatever you're threatening, and like a provoked snake, they lash out.

DEPERSONALIZE THE ATTACK. It's not *you* they're after. It's what you represent. It feels personal, but it's not. If someone else were in your shoes, they'd be the one with the arrow in the back.

STAND BY YOUR CONVICTIONS. If you're following your vision, doing things legally and ethically, and even helping people and someone still objects, they are really telling you that they don't share your values. In fact, some entrepreneurs tell us that it's only after someone comes gunning for them that they feel truly successful and connected to their values.

THINK LIKE A FREEDOM FIGHTER—you know, like Elliot Alderson in *Mr. Robot.* Anticipate sabotage and prepare your counterattack before it happens. That could mean having an emergency fund, finding a great crisis publicist, or building healthy alliances with respected people who will join your charge.

Assume that things won't go smoothly, and then you can be pleasantly surprised when they do.

5

RIGHT A GREAT WRONG

In the 1952 novel *East of Eden*, author John Steinbeck wrote that "humans are caught . . . in a net of good and evil," and after someone "has brushed off the dust and chips of life," only "the hard, clean questions" will remain: "Was it good or was it evil? Have I done well—or ill?"

Moral and ethical dilemmas are all around us. The debate between right and wrong, good and bad, has existed for centuries. As humanist Bill Haines puts it, "We define 'right' as that which tends to maximize human happiness, and 'wrong' as that which tends to maximize human misery."

According to some psychologists and primatologists, we are born with a moral grammar that provides us with the ability to generate moral judgment, or an innate sense of right and wrong. Ethics are a set of principles developed purposefully over time while "morality is not just something that people learn," argues Yale psychologist Paul Bloom, but rather "something we are all born with."

At many points in life, we'll come face to face with varying degrees of social injustice, including harassment, inequality, marginalization, racism, or hate. Some of us choose to take a stand against those injustices. Rebellions thrive on righteous rage, resentment against power, hope for a better future. Sometimes, the facts aren't enough to motivate us to step out of our safe, cozy cubicles and throw down with a company or a government, even when we know it's the right thing to do.

That's the plot of countless movies. Someone commits an evil act, moving the hero to do outrageous things and take great risks to balance the scales. That same impulse is what also compels some people to rebel against a broken system. The hunger for "what's right" can make us do all sorts of things that on the surface seem crazy.

And that's what Matt Scanlan did.

› Naadam Cashmere

Scanlan made his crazy decision in 2014 under the strangest of circumstances. He had been a rebel since his earliest days: getting kicked out of school for drinking, learning to pass his exams by befriending the smartest kids in class (or even the teacher), and quitting NYU but somehow still ending up with a job on Wall Street at age twenty-two. In other words, he has always been somebody who had no use for the well-trodden path.

But Scanlan hated Wall Street, so he quit his job, and went to Mongolia with a friend. After a seemingly endless series of flights and an all-day drive, he found himself in one of the most remote locations in the world. The place fascinated him, so he stayed for a month. He ate the food, drank goat's milk vodka, and got to know the nomadic people and their ancient culture. What he learned both moved and infuriated him.

The area's economy was built around raising Zalaa Jinst White goats, which produce the finest cashmere wool in the world, but it was so remote that wool buyers came around only once a season.

When they did, they paid the herders a pittance and then resold the wool through a daisy chain of agents for a ridiculous markup. The native herders were being paid so poorly that they lived in poverty. Hundreds of thousands of families had already moved to the capital, Ulaanbaatar, to take better-paying mining jobs. The situation put a three-thousand-year-old culture in danger of dying out.

The injustice brought out Scanlan's inner rebel—the one who had been expelled from school years earlier and was itching to stir something up. In true Rare Breed fashion, rather than just blowing something up and calling the job done, he decided to use his frustration with the circumstances to disrupt the exploitative cashmere supply chain with a socially conscious cashmere apparel brand that pays herders a fair price for their product. He knew nothing about the wool business, but minor obstacles like that don't stop Rare Breeds. In 2015, he returned to the Gobi Desert, carrying $2.5 million in cash in grocery bags like a character from *Breaking Bad*. Matt bought 150 tons of top-quality wool for a fair price and launched Naadam (pronounced NAH-dum), named after a celebratory Mongolian festival.

Today, Naadam pays Mongolian herders 50 percent more than traditional dealers; charges the customer 50 percent less; runs a green business; has established a nonprofit organization that provides herders with veterinary programs, livestock insurance, and breeding support; has broken the cashmere cartel; and manages to produce some of the finest cashmere clothes on the planet.

› How to Own This Mantra

Turning a cause into the backbone of your business is one way to make your business matter. But first, you need to discover your cause. What issues do you care about? What great wrong in the world tugs at the hem of *your* soul? It could be about race, gender, animal rights, bullying, homelessness, fashion, health, the voting system, climate change—whatever your fancy. Figure out what triggers you to say "I cannot fucking believe this is happening!" Something that keeps you up at night. Something you *have* to get your hands on. Often, your cause finds you, so get out there and experience as much life as you can in as many places as you can. Matt Scanlan found his cause in the Gobi Desert.

Here are a few things to think about:

RECRUIT FELLOW REBELS WITH A CAUSE. No revolution happens because of just one person. Get on Kickstarter, Indiegogo, or Peerbackers and find people who are in love with your idea and will back you. Publish your personal manifesto on Medium and let your vision attract others who think like you do. Grab apps like Shapr or Happening and start expanding your tribe.

MAKE IT A WIN-WIN. Everyone in the chain should benefit—the business owner, customer, and supplier. In other words, whatever or whoever you're fighting for should benefit just as much as you do.

DON'T JUST TALK, ACT. The most important secret to success in any discipline is simply taking action. How many people do you know who are all talk and don't *do* anything? Change requires more than words. In order to make a dent, or disrupt, you've got to make the injustice obsolete. Scanlan didn't wait ten years to seize the opportunity. He went and made it happen.

TRACK YOUR IMPACT. Look at how many hours you've served, how many lives you've changed, and what outcomes you've achieved. Analyze how you've impacted the lives of beneficiaries, stakeholders, employees, and partnerships to improve people, processes, and the planet, and then put numbers to it. For example, Naadam helped found and manages the Gobi Revival Fund, which supports one thousand nomadic herding families in Mongolia and in two years provided veterinary care to more than 250,000 goats. Brands like Starbucks,

Timberland, and Patagonia all have corporate social responsibility (CSR) or corporate responsibility (CR) reports, which are used to measure and improve the impact of their programs.

Oh, one last thought: Don't get it twisted. Righting a great wrong shouldn't be about revenge—it's about restoring the moral balance.

6

PRACTICE QUIET COURAGE

> Courage does not always roar. Sometimes courage is the quiet voice at the end of the day saying, "I will try again tomorrow."
>
> **—Mary Anne Radmacher**

We think of rebels and rebellions as big booms—bold and boisterous. When there's injustice or someone is exploiting people, we all expect someone to rush in and make a ruckus, because let's face it, it's cathartic to see a rebel kick up the dust. But not all rebellious acts get an anthem, and not all courage needs to be loud. There is another subtle type of courage that is every bit as transformative for people, businesses, and communities. It is *quiet courage.*

For you quietly rebellious Rare Breeds, your calling card isn't something that gets splashed across the front page of the *New York Times.* Instead, your Mantra is about embracing your unique style of defiance. Small acts that fly under the radar can still wind up making a world of difference.

For example, when talking about women's suffrage, the history books justifiably focus on outspoken leaders. But there were also quieter, often overlooked acts that helped get women the vote. For the Nineteenth Amendment to be ratified, thirty-six states had to approve it. Tennessee was No. 36, and a first-term state legislator named Harry Burn was the deciding vote. He was planning to vote no—until his mother sent him a letter and told him, "don't forget to be a good boy" and to "vote for Suffrage." That small nudge flipped him from a no to a yes, the amendment passed, and history changed.

There's also the remarkable story of Sadako Sasaki, a Japanese girl whose brief life spawned a timeless tradition of folding origami cranes to heal the world. At just two years old, Sasaki was exposed to radiation when the United States dropped the atomic bomb on Hiroshima. As a result, she developed leukemia by the age of twelve. During her long hospital stays, Sasaki folded origami paper cranes, inspired by the Japanese legend that a person who created a thousand origami cranes would be granted a wish. Her wish was simply to live.

Her older brother Masahiro Sasaki, who speaks on his sister's life at events, said that Sadako exceeded her goal and folded approximately fourteen hundred paper cranes before she died, each one representing a quiet act of rebellion and courage. Her legacy lives on, and cranes have become a symbol of peace. The family has donated some of Sadako's cranes to important places around the world: in New York City to the 9/11 memorial, to the Pearl Harbor Visitor Center, to the Truman Library and Museum, and to the Museum of Tolerance in Los Angeles.

To be a Rare Breed, the spirit of fighting for something must be in your blood. But you might be overwhelmed by the idea that making a difference means doing something huge and complicated. If that's keeping you from ruffling a few feathers, we have good news. Acts of resistance and defiance are often subtle. Apply them in the right place and at the right time, and even seemingly small acts can go on to change everything.

› The Diplomat Who Saved Thousands of Jews

Meet Chiune Sugihara, hailed as a hero in his native Japan. Owner of a lifelong rebellious streak, he entered the diplomatic corps to see the world and in 1939 was assigned to run the Japanese consulate in Lithuania.

At that time, Germany under Hitler had occupied Poland, nations around the world had declared war, and Jews were fleeing Nazi-run territories for their lives. Many of them wound up at Sugihara's embassy, desperate for visas that would allow them to travel through Japan to other parts of the world where they would be safe from genocide. However, despite his many pleas, Sugihara's superiors instructed him not to issue any visas to the Jewish refugees.

After consulting with his wife, and fully aware that he was ending his diplomatic career, Sugihara began issuing visas anyway—handwriting them around the clock, sometimes hundreds in a single day, until his wife had to massage his aching hands. Years later, when asked about his actions, Sugihara was matter-of-fact. He'd simply had no choice. "We had thousands of people hanging around the windows of our residence. There was no other way," he said.

When the consulate closed in 1940, Sugihara was out of a job and according to the *New York Times* his visas had "no legal standing," but he took consulate stationery and an official stamp with him and kept writing visas that persuaded officials to allow families to travel freely. The US Holocaust Memorial Museum reports that Sugihara wrote visas for 2,140 people, which also covered some 300 family members, mostly children.

Sugihara wasn't flamboyant or wealthy or dramatic. He was a man who couldn't look away from an injustice, and he had the means at hand to do something small—a quiet, subtle act of resistance paired with a ridiculous amount of courage that could, and did, change the future for thousands of families.

In 2017, the Tokyo Weekender asked five hundred residents of Japan's capital to nominate their candidate for the "Greatest Japanese Person Ever." It wasn't the name of a revolutionary, monarch, or baseball star. It was Chiune Sugihara.

› How to Own This Mantra

Quiet courage is the acts you take when no one's watching. It's doing something that you're scared to do—something your body is telling you not to do—and doing it anyway. Sometimes there is no immediate reward, no standing ovation, pat on the back, or reassuring words.

Here's what you can do:

GO SMALL. If your inner voice is saying "Be defiant" but you don't have the personality for it, take a small step. Confetti didn't fall when Rosa Parks quietly refused to give up her bus seat the evening of December 1, 1955. She didn't pound the seats or throw a tantrum. It was one soundless act of courage that changed segregation in the United States forever.

Maybe you feel like you can't do much in this world because you're one person and you don't have millions of dollars. Stop right there. Every single one of us can have an impact. You have power, and when you drop the idea that rebellion has to mean organizing a Million Something March, you can start using that power.

THINK ABOUT LEVERS OF POWER. What if you can identify them and move them up, down, left, or right? What micro move makes a big difference? Chiune Sugihara didn't have to change Japanese politics or fight Hitler to save thousands of Jews; he knew that if he wrote visas without permission, thousands of people would be able to escape before his bosses caught on. He identified the right lever and pulled it.

PRACTICE ACTS OF BRAVERY. Being brave is refusing to engage in gossip, standing up to a bully, asking for something you might not get, or taking in an abused animal. Courage is a habit, it's something you can practice; and the more you do it, the better you'll get. As the theologian Mary Daly said, "You learn courage by couraging."

VIRTUE 2

AUDACIOUS

Bold. Ambitious. Visionary. Unstoppable. Daring.

An asset when unshakable conviction in a crazy vision unlocks futures that don't exist and inspires people to attempt the impossible.

A weakness when egotism breeds a reckless disregard for reality and the inability to acknowledge one's shortcomings.

In early 2007, when Motto was trying to kick off its training wheels, we drove to Atlanta to take our shot in a high-profile women's business event. Thousands of entries from around the country had been narrowed to nine female entrepreneurs, us included, who would each pitch their business models to a panel of superstar judges. The prize package was no joke: a generous line of credit from AMEX and marketing, mentoring, and technology resources. We were coming from a 150-square-foot room and barely making ends meet—this was our entrepreneurial dream come true.

The day before the live event, Ashleigh swaggered up to the podium for our practice pitch, and in front of some of the smartest, most accomplished women in the country . . . she totally went blank. She forgot our names, what we did, and what we had accomplished. After a few agonizing seconds, a judge infamous for withering critiques tore her apart with a few words that stung like hell. Ashleigh fled the stage, humiliated. It was such an epic fail in such a high-pressure situation that everyone assumed we wouldn't be back the next day to make the actual pitch.

Drowning our sorrows in the hotel bar, we cried, cursed, drunk-texted, cursed some more, and played a ton of sad songs on the jukebox as we questioned our worth. There we were, the youngest women in the competition, getting our shot at the heavyweight title, and we'd been knocked out in the first round. And not just by anyone, but by the Floyd Mayweather of female entrepreneurship. We might have been gutsy on the outside, but at the first sign of adversity, we'd folded like lawn chairs.

Then, as we packed our bags for an early trip home, we looked at each other and had the same thought. *Oh hell no! We* want *this. We are not leaving. We can't slink away with our tails between our legs.* That was what the judges were expecting. But we would at least go down fighting. It was a bold move, given that we'd been torn to shreds a few hours earlier, but it was the attitude that had gotten us there in the first place. We hadn't taken criticism as a hard no in the past, so why start now?

So, we stayed up all night, rewrote our pitch on bar napkins, went in the next morning, and crushed the pitch. That's right, Ashleigh won the whole damn thing and became the youngest winner of Count Me In's Make Mine a Million $ Business award.

Those same brutal, unforgiving judges gave us a standing ovation in front of hundreds of people. It never would have happened if we hadn't had the audacity to prove them wrong.

› Daring to Do What Others Won't

Audacity is a cocktail of nerve, radical vision, and unshakable self-confidence. It's having the guts and vision to see possibility where others see boundaries. You go where others won't and happily consider the risk without an ounce of hesitation; you have no shame in tossing out ideas that make people shake their heads in disbelief. They look at you like you've gone around the bend. And you *love* it.

You're like a valiant, underweight boxer constantly climbing in the ring with bloodthirsty opponents twice your size. You stand in your corner alone, shadow boxing, while your opponent—which could be a multibillion-dollar corporation, a stubborn social norm, or the sound barrier—mocks you. The crowd assumes it will be a slaughter . . . until the bell rings.

Audacity is Stanford University PhD students Larry Page and Sergey Brin deciding in 1996 that search technology sucked and setting out to organize the world's information in a way that would make it accessible to anyone with an internet connection. That, of course, became Google.

Audacity is test pilot Geraldyn Cobb and the Mercury 13 women, who launched a national conversation about gender discrimination in the spaceflight industry after surpassing qualifying tests to become astronauts, but never making it to space. It's thousands of women staring down Harvey Weinstein and setting the #MeToo wildfire.

Audacious individuals are emissaries from a world that doesn't yet exist but *will.* Many of history's great inflection points probably never would have happened without them, because every idea is called stupid and impractical until somebody has the vision and courage to get down in the dirt and make something out of the mud pie.

There was Galileo, who birthed modern science when he confronted the Catholic hierarchy with evidence to support Copernicus's blasphemous finding that the earth went around the sun. The twentieth century brought us Virginia Hall, one of the most daring and effective Allied spies of World War II. She ran safe houses, assisted the French resistance, and scaled the Pyrenees to escape Nazi pursuers—all despite having a wooden leg. Now, that's a badass! There was Amelia Earhart, who proved that a woman aviator could be the equal of any man and did it with panache.

Today, audacious minds include Amanda de Cadenet, who realized that magazine photography was an all-white male world and turned her response to that—#Girlgaze—into a creative agency and a movement; Tali Gumbiner and Lizzie Wilson, advertising creative directors who took a risk to promote their Wall Street client by installing Fearless Girl, a bronze figure in a power pose, right in front of Wall Street's famous Charging Bull, and helped their client boost business by 400 percent; Elon Musk, who smoked weed during a live interview on the Joe Rogan Experience because, who the fuck knows?; and Charlamagne Tha God, who grew up dreaming of life beyond a dirt road in South Carolina and believed he could be one of the biggest multimedia personalities in the world.

Great minds are audacious as fuck. Most of all, they do the unthinkable and leave the existing state of affairs unsettled and shaking.

› The Notorious RBG

If you don't think a five-foot-one-inch, eighty-six-year-old woman can be audacious, you haven't met Ruth Bader Ginsburg. Before she was the "Notorious RBG," a SCOTUS justice, a feminist folk hero, and the face that launched a thousand memes, she was a quiet trailblazer and one of nine women at Harvard Law. That might not sound particularly bold to us now, but it was in the 1950s: this was a place where an administrator once asked her, "How do you justify taking a spot from a qualified man?" *Please.*

RBG's quiet but relentless resoluteness continued as she started her professional life. Facing gender discrimination on the job market, she ended up working for the ACLU, where she cofounded the Women's Rights Project. She became Columbia Law School's first tenured female professor, and in 1993 President Bill Clinton nominated her to be on the Supreme Court.

There she began an illustrious career of schooling the majority with brilliant, blistering dissents and taking the lead in landmark decisions ranging from overturning male-only university admissions to the Lilly Ledbetter Fair Pay Act of 2009. But what makes RBG a model of audacity is that at eighty-six, an age when most women would be taking a victory lap, she continues to speak out, not just for feminism and freedom, but for harmony. That's an act of valor worth a thousand stories.

This quotation illustrates her spirit perfectly: "Fight for the things that you care about but do it in a way that will lead others to join you." RBG isn't the hero we deserve, but she's the hero we need. Plus, she looks like a total boss in a sequin-studded judicial collar.

› Audacity Is a Calling

No one chooses to be audacious. It chooses *you* when an idea lands on your brain like a dandelion seed on a dew-drenched lawn and immediately starts to grow. But it's not a dandelion; it's an invading organism like kudzu. Let it put down roots and its tendrils quickly strangle everything you thought you wanted to do. All that's left is an indistinct shape draped in layers of vines, something that you feel responsible for bringing into being.

Just like that, you've been called.

If you don't answer, you might regret it for the rest of your life.

Audacity is about advocating for a future that doesn't yet exist. You have a vision of a world that can be, *should* be, *must* be, shimmering in front of your eyes. It's the prime mover behind everything you do, everyone you work with, and everything you think, write, and say. Some people might see parts of the picture, because visionaries always attract disciples. But nobody but you will ever see or comprehend it all. Prophets don't get peers. Jesus didn't have a co-messiah. Audacity can be *lonely*.

Audacity comes with plenty of upside, too. You've got a secret. You're the only one who knows the full story behind the next smart device, bionic implant, or cryptocurrency. You have ringside seats to something with a puncher's chance of turning part of the world upside down, and that's the kind of thrill ride that makes you do what you do. As the great Roman Stoic philosopher Seneca reminds us, "*Non est ad astra mollis e terris via*," which means "There is no easy way from the earth to the stars."

> All I got is dreams, nobody else believes.
>
> **—Jay-Z, "History"**

› Audacity Is a Secret Weapon

Audacious Rare Breeds are creators. They dream about raising their batons and hearing the cosmos play the tune that's in their hearts. Whether you use silicon, ink, or concrete to breathe life into something that once existed only in your mind, you're conducting the music of the spheres.

Ever been part of something run by an audacious lunatic? It's crazy-making and energizing at the same time. You're working harder than ever, but you don't mind because you're making history while others are spectating. You have no idea whether what you're doing will reinvent part of the world or end up a cautionary tale, and it doesn't matter.

But the coolest thing is that audacity *scales*. Maybe you made the small but bold move to offer a controversial perspective in a meeting rather than sitting quietly on the sidelines. It seems minor, but that small move was daring, and it's priming you for bigger opportunities.

Whether you're a visionary graffiti artist or a talented backup dancer for J. Lo who wants to get out of the shadows and show the world what you've got, you're already audacious. You have to be to even think about breaking free of a traditional career.

But don't just *think* audacious; *be* audacious.

Like J. Kevin White. In 2005, he was director of humanitarian assistance for the Department of Defense for Africa and Eastern Europe, watching the poor in Morocco accept donated eyeglasses. Great idea, except that most people chose the glasses on the basis of their frames, not whether they corrected their eyesight. Ninety percent of the specs became trash.

The average Joe shrugs and says, "What a shame." But White responded with something bolder than that. He launched Global Vision 2020 and invented the USee refractometer, which uses sliding lens strips to allow aid workers in the field to quickly and accurately diagnose vision problems and prescribe corrective lenses—which they provide on the spot with a mobile kit. Global Vision 2020 is helping needy people see better in seven countries and counting.

As White says, "I'm just a Marine who saw a problem, had an idea, and said 'Someone needs to do something about this. And when no one did, I said 'Okay, I'll give it a try.'"

Audacity can be that simple.

> At the very moment when people underestimate you is when you can make a breakthrough.
>
> —Germany Kent

› You Need Audacity to Grow

You know all of those super-successful people and companies that play it safe and never change lanes? Oh, you've never heard of them? That's because they don't *exist*. People who lack the moxie to stick their necks out become irrelevant.

If you're a child of the 1980s, you remember Blockbuster Video fondly. Piling into a car on a Saturday night, rummaging through the movie rental store's shelves, marveling at some of the horrible direct-to-DVD movies that got produced—it was fun. If you're too young to remember Blockbuster, then you missed an era.

Blockbuster was the $4 billion big dog in home video until a little upstart named Netflix came along and started mailing people DVDs. Blockbuster ignored them and passed on the opportunity to buy Netflix in the early 2000s for a mere $50 million. Blockbuster's CEO didn't have the vision to see where home entertainment was going—streaming—and lacked the audacity to take a risk. That was the beginning of the end. Today, Netflix is worth about $150 billion and owns streaming entertainment. Blockbuster went bankrupt in 2010.

It takes nerve to continue reinventing a business, especially when you've settled into a nice, profitable groove. But the key word is *settled.* When you settle, you stop moving, and stationary targets are easy to hit. Competitors come after you, improve on what you've done, blow past you, and before you know it, you're mediocre. Worried you'll reach too far and fail? Name a single great entrepreneur or innovator who hasn't failed miserably. *You can't.* In one of Fred Astaire's first screen tests, notes were made like, "Can't sing. Can't act. Slightly balding. Can dance a little." Lady Gaga got dropped by Island Def Jam records after three months. Oprah was fired from her gig as a reporter at a Baltimore TV station. Failure and audacity are two sides of the same coin.

Of course, the ridiculous risks that sometimes lead to failure also produce big wins, and that's why audacity is in the DNA of every great entrepreneur, leader, and disruptor. It's your growth engine. Without it, you go nowhere.

This is true beyond the boardroom. How do you get the date with that special someone you've been flirting with and thinking about for weeks? Risk rejection and ask that person out. How do you start working out when you haven't exercised since high school PE? Take that hip hop dance class, even if it means embarrassing the hell out of yourself.

How can you force the action? How can you reach beyond your grasp over and over again? How can you make that leap from "I'd like to do this" to "I'm actually doing this"? Those are the questions that bold, audacious, throw-caution-to-the-wind leaders ask. And as an aspiring leader or entrepreneur, those are the questions you should ask too.

> You see things; and you say "Why?" But I dream things that never were; and I say "Why not?"
>
> **—George Bernard Shaw, *Back to Methuselah***

› The Dark Side of Audacity

But when audacity spirals into reckless hubris, it becomes destructive. If anything exemplifies this, it's the Greek myth of Icarus. He and his father Daedalus are imprisoned on the island of Crete. Daedalus builds two sets of wings made of feathers and wax so they can escape, but he cautions his son, *Don't fly too close to the sun or your wings will melt.* Of course, Icarus ignores his father's warnings, decides he has to soar higher than the birds, and plunges into the sea.

Tempering audacity with caution and wisdom will help you avoid taking the wrong kind of risks. It's all about balance. Fly too low and you'll play it too safe and squander your potential. You don't want to be Ferdinand Foch, a French general during World War I who, clearly not getting the potential of aviation, said in 1911, "Airplanes are interesting scientific toys, but they are of no military value." But fly too high and arrogance will alienate your friends and crush your plans. You don't want to be Billy McFarland, whose vision of creating a first-of-its-kind live music fantasy for the One Percent birthed the Fyre Festival, but whose stubbornness and refusal to accept reality led to disaster—thousands stranded in the middle of nowhere, charges of massive fraud—all playing out live on social media.

Audacity is about doing bold things and moving the world forward, not scratching a narcissistic itch or trying to make the world buzz about your genius. Don Hambrick, a professor at Penn State University Smeal College of Business, and coauthor Arijit Chatterjee conducted two extensive studies of leaders in the tech sector ("Executive Personality, Capability Cues, and Risk Taking: How Narcissistic CEOs React to Their Successes and Stumbles" and "It's All About Me: Narcissistic Chief Executive Officers and Their Effects on Company Strategy and Performance") to find out the effect that hubristic leaders have on their companies. The answer is, *Not a good one.* Companies run by leaders who scored high in four characteristics of narcissism—entitlement, insistence on being the center of attention, arrogance, and self-admiration—were more likely to waste money, make expensive acquisitions, and have extreme ups and downs in performance. In other words, they tend to dangle their companies and their people over the edge of ruin so they can feel good about themselves. Basically, don't be that leader.

› Putting Audacity to Work

Being bold isn't always popular at first. That's why a saying often attributed to philosopher Arthur Schopenhauer goes like this: "All truth passes through three stages. First, it is ridiculed. Second, it is violently opposed. Third, it is accepted as being self-evident."

You can safely assume that whatever you do, tons of people will be offended by you. Don't let that stop you, but also don't let it surprise you when someone tells you (to your face or behind your back) how irked they are by your very being.

Being an audacious Rare Breed means that for all the people who walk away from you bewildered by your absurdity, twice as many will be (often silently) drawn to your ideas and chutzpah. They'll be inspired by you, and you by them. Embracing audacity prunes away the false friends who'd rather watch you crash than see you do what they didn't have the courage to try. That makes more room for allies who will support you.

Without further ado, here are three questions that will help you extract the greatest benefit from your spectacular audacity:

1. WHAT WOULD I DO WITH MY CAREER OR BUSINESS IF I KNEW THERE WERE NO LIMITS?

One of the biggest obstacles we face in pushing ourselves beyond the confines of our daily life is, well . . . us. Instead of taking a leap, we dream up a plethora of roadblocks such as, "It's not the right time. There's no money. We've got kids, bills, loans, dogs, hamsters, etc." These all may be true, but you do have options. They just may not be *easy* options. You will never change your life and become a Rare Breed believing your dreams are too far out of your reach. Pursue your life with reckless abandon. Why wouldn't you?

2. AM I WILLING TO PUSH HARDER WHEN I GET TO THE TOP?

Being audacious is like being possessed by a voice that shouts, "Make this happen! Bring this into being!" and doing whatever it takes to follow that voice. That's how you become Tiger Woods, the best golf player of his era. Throughout his career, Tiger continuously changed and rebuilt his golf swing to get better in order to stay at the top. There are plenty of one-trick players who have won the green jacket but never go on to win anything again. To be audacious like Tiger, you have to continuously improve or you won't be on top for long.

3. WHAT HAPPENS IF I FAIL?

Audacious plans fail sometimes; that's reality. But don't fear. Failure leaves cool scars. Remember, the failure of a brave proposal is no failure at all unless you make it one by throwing in the towel or deciding you don't have what it takes.

The following Mantras offer lessons every audacious Rare Breed needs to hear. Everyone featured in them chose to leverage the power of their audacity, faced ridicule and misunderstanding, but charged on anyway. Let their audacious triumphs be a road map for yours.

7

DO WHAT CAN'T BE DONE

Impossible is just a big word thrown around by small men who find it easier to live in the world they've been given than to explore the power they have to change it. Impossible is not a fact. It's an opinion. Impossible is not a declaration. It's a dare. Impossible is potential. Impossible is temporary. Impossible is nothing.

—Aimee Lehto Schewe

This isn't the first version of *Rare Breed* we tried to publish. Once, we had a slightly different book in mind, but every publisher we submitted it to rejected it. As each rejection letter rolled in, our hearts sank a little more.

"Hansberger and Bonnell are impressive—and they clearly know of what they write—but I have concerns about a book on branding."

"These authors are so impressive and accomplished (esp for their age!). It's really just the CMO audience who would read a book like this—and that's a much smaller audience. I just don't think this is the ideal fit for us. Regrettably it's a no."

"Sorry, this isn't a fit. Branding books just don't sell."

"Thought the material was fresh, but we've had trouble selling branding books in the past. Sorry, but it's a no. The girls sure are incredible though."

"No thanks, but thanks for thinking of us."

There were at least fifteen more like that, and we tacked each one up in our office until we were surrounded by the platitudes of defeat. Crushed emotionally, spiritually, and mentally, we shoved our book proposal into a box and didn't speak of it again for a while.

Six months later, we got a call from our dear friend and mentor Mark Levy. Mark is a high-energy, outspoken, genius consultant; a bestselling author; a persuasion expert; and has worked with the most acclaimed thought leaders, authors, and celebrities in the world. Oh, and he's a renowned magician, which we'll talk about later in chapter 33. Mark has literally watched us grow up. He was the first consultant we scrounged up enough money to hire in our early twenties, and twelve years later, he helped us refine the concept of Rare Breed.

"What happened?" he said.

"We don't know," we sighed. "It got rejected."

We're not going to lie: we were feeling pretty lost and must've looked like two sad stray dogs on our Skype call. Instantly, Mark thrust his face forward, practically squishing it against his monitor, and said, "WHAT?! Are you *kidding* me? The concept of Rare Breed is fucking *BRILLIANT*! Go rewrite it."

We recoiled, looked at each other, and then grinned. Mark's boot in the ass was the shot in the arm we needed, just like Sunny's dad had given us a kick and a cuddle a few years before. We hauled our manuscript out of the box, brushed away the cobwebs, and started over. Suddenly, it was clear: the concept was great, but we had *positioned* it wrong. *Rare Breed* wasn't a branding book; it was a personal growth book for ambitious entrepreneurs, leaders, creators, and provocateurs.

Within twenty-four hours, we were back at the computer, staring at a blank cursor. We took the premise of the book down to the studs and refined the concept on the basis of our experience—on how personal traits that other people call vices are actually the Virtues that can lead to success.

There was just one, small snag.

The title.

Everybody in the book world, including our agent, told us we were wasting our time going back to publishers with the same title: *Rare Breed*. "It can't be done," we heard over and over again. "It's foolish. Just go sell the book under a different name," another adviser quipped. Acquisitions editors, the people who make the decision to buy a book, would see the title again and reject the project out of hand, we were told. But we believed in our title and refused to change it, because we don't believe in impossible. Hard? Sure. But not impossible.

So, *Rare Breed* made its way to acquisitions editors again—same title, sharper concept. And obviously, the fact that you're reading these words right now is proof that the experts were wrong. Having the audacity to believe this book would be published, despite everyone telling us that it couldn't be done, is why it's in your hands. Throughout the process, people called us dangerous, difficult, and defiant—

essentially the very essence of this book—but we could see what they *couldn't* and knew it was the right path to take.

So, the next time you're feeling low because an audition didn't go your way or your new idea didn't get funded, pick up this book. It's a reminder that nothing is impossible.

Life is one giant invitation.

› Impossible Burger

It's only human to limit our belief in what's possible to what's in front of our eyes. But we also know that at one time, flying machines and handheld devices that contain all the world's knowledge were fantasies. Those advances and thousands of others like them came about because in response to being told "It can't be done," someone said, "Says who?"

Audacious people think in terms of what's possible, not what's impossible. If you're audacious, you don't need the comfort of believing that the world has all been explained. You love the fact that there's still so much to figure out, shadowy corners yet to be explored, deep oceans hiding the unknown, and epic challenges to test your will and your endurance. You see the word *impossible* as a challenge, not a verdict.

Impossible is what Patrick Brown heard when everybody told him that making a plant-based meat patty with no animal ingredients that would smell, look, and taste like beef couldn't be done. If you've ever tried to eat a veggie burger and watched it fall apart in your hands, you probably agree. Sad face.

Brown was acutely aware of the toll that animal agriculture around the world exacted on the environment: water pollution, forest degradation, wildlife extinction, massive greenhouse gas production. He was determined to make the global food system more sustainable, and as a physician and biochemist, he had the brains to do so.

So, he innovated. He figured out that it wasn't just the taste that made carnivores love beef but the smell, the texture, and the fact that it *bleeds*. After much experimentation, he found the magic ingredient—an isolated pigment from hemoglobin called *heme*, which gives blood its color and cooked meat its distinctive smell and flavor. After exhaustive trial and error (he writes on his blog that his flavor team compared one early prototype burger to rancid polenta), Brown combined heme, wheat protein, potato protein paste, coconut oil, and voilà! Impossible Burger was born.

Today, Brown's Impossible products are sold in more than fourteen hundred restaurants, his company has attracted more than $300 million in funding, and he's scaring the faces off the beef industry. It's a pretty bold move to create a high-tech, eco-friendly burger that can make meat eaters salivate. Brown could have tackled the problems of raising and eating cattle in a way that was less taxing and not tried to change the entire meatless burger industry. But he knew what we (and you) know: most of us don't really find that next gear unless everything is at . . . *steak*. Sorry, we just couldn't resist a terrible beef pun.

And yes, the Impossible Burger really does smell, taste, and bleed like a beef burger. Try one and send us photos of you eating it in disbelief.

› How to Own This Mantra

Doing what can't be done means having a short memory. You've got to be able to look your defeats right in the eye, extract the lessons they have to teach you, and then forget about those defeats. Never accept a defeat as a judgment, because it's not. It's just one episode in your story.

Prepare for the impossible now. Assume you're going to fail (because everyone does) and surround yourself with things and people who will pick you up and remind you who you are and what you're capable of. We had Mark Levy.

Where to start?

BUILD AN "IMPOSSIBILITY AIRBAG." Fill it with all the stuff you'll need to cushion the blow when you fall on your ass: friends, butt-kicking mentors, encouraging notes, links to Lifehack stories or famous quotations about failure leading to success, video messages to yourself about getting back up after a defeat—and very possibly, wine and chocolate (chocolate is optional). Failure burns, and it's okay to wallow for a bit. But only for a bit. Then, back to work.

UNDERSTAND THAT ACHIEVING THE IMPOSSIBLE IS A COMMITMENT. You can't commit to try. You must commit to succeed—simple as that.

AIM HIGHER THAN COMMON SENSE SUGGESTS. Go for the job or goal that you're *hungry* for, not the one that offers the path of least resistance. If you're leading a company, steer toward the high-risk venture or the entrenched competitor. If you're a freelancer, go after the gig that will make you one of the elite, not just the gig that pays the bills.

RESEARCH TO FIND GAPS OR OPPORTUNITIES. Scour old journals, try products, learn how things are made and why they are made a certain way. Half the battle of doing the impossible is catching the oversight of others. Research other categories and industries outside your focus to connect the dots. Find out what approaches didn't work and go for extreme or unorthodox methods.

PARTNER WITH EXPERTS OR INTERN WITH THEM. You might not be a master of every discipline you need in order to do the impossible. But you can reach out and build a team of experts. Or, you can intern or study with the greatest thinkers in a specific category or field, like

Patrick Brown—he connected with nutritionists, nutraceuticals experts, and beef and plant experts.

PLAN ON LOTS OF FUCK-UPS. Brown made a lot of terrible-tasting burgers before he got a winner, and you're going to do the same. Every time you build a prototype that fails, you've just eliminated one more wrong way to reach your goal.

Above all, remember that when someone says something is impossible, what they're really saying is, "That's impossible for me."

8

DRIVE THE HORSES INTO THE SEA

Before the invention of the steamship and rail travel, cargo got from one side of the world to the other by sailing vessel. In those days of wooden ships and iron men, ships would ply the trade winds of the Atlantic Ocean and brave the dangerous passage near Cape Horn carrying hides, tobacco, and other goods.

Such travel was slow and difficult, so sailors learned the areas of the sea to avoid. One was known as the "horse latitudes," two zones of high barometric pressure and calm winds extending about thirty degrees north and south of the Equator in the Atlantic. Ships caught in these areas could lose the winds they needed to make headway and flounder for days, even weeks, running dangerously low on drinking water and food.

One of the stories about how these parts of the ocean got their name has to do with the many horses allegedly sacrificed in those waters. You see, if a vessel carried horses (as many did), the desperate sailors were sometimes forced to drive the horses overboard so they would not drink water that the crew needed to stay alive. There was no second thought, no hesitation. It needed to be done.

Imagine listening to those horses, terrified and screaming, as they grew weaker and slipped beneath the waves. How strong and dedicated a captain would you have to be to make that brutal decision?

Throughout your career, you too will have to make the hard calls. You might find that something or someone you care about is holding you back. It might be an employee you adore who isn't getting the job done, a client who's fun to work with but doesn't pay his or her bills, or a piece of work that you shed blood over that doesn't fit the strategy anymore. In other words, you might have to kill your darlings if they're holding you back.

› Sacrifice Is Necessary

Recently, we conducted our signature workshop for a client in the animated film business during which we did a deep dive on the company. While interviewing a C-Suite exec, he told us a fascinating true story about sacrificing for the greater good.

While making *Beauty and the Beast*, Disney's production team identified a major issue at the tail end of production: the story didn't have enough breathing room to develop the love between Belle and the Beast. In that version of the film, the "Be Our Guest" song was sung to Belle's father Maurice, who was in the castle much longer before being imprisoned. When the team realized that the sequence didn't work, they made the decision to scrap it and rework it so that Maurice was tossed in a cell immediately, Belle arrived much sooner, and the song was sung to her instead. This gave Belle, the Beast, and his servants the screen time they needed to tell a better story. The film went on to be the first full-length animated film to be nominated for the Academy Award for Best Picture.

The core Mantra Disney embedded into its team was that any idea that makes a movie better is worth doing, even if it will cost more time or money, slows you down, or makes you redo what you've already done. That sequence was their horse. They threw it overboard to make the most amazing movie possible.

We practice this Mantra all the time. In fact, while developing our Rare Breed content and video series, we had all kinds of horses. We went through *six* teams and recorded *ten* episodes before realizing that the entire format of the show and the crew working on it didn't match our vision. We spent tens of thousands of dollars and months of planning, shooting, and agonizing over every detail, only to throw it all away. We had to kill those ideas so we could refocus on the right ones. We finally forged ahead, found the right team, produced our first episode with Charlamagne Tha God, and nailed it.

> How to Own This Mantra

Think of your horses as ideas or work you're most proud of, something that you love, that you've spent time nurturing. Now imagine driving those same horses over the side of your ship because you know that keeping them will slow you down or starve your business. (Please don't come for us, PETA—it's just a metaphor!)

Audacious leaders know that they have to sacrifice whatever prevents them from getting to the promised land. Falling too in love with your own ideas can blind you, stall innovation, and even lead you away from the problem you hoped to solve. If an idea doesn't serve the greater good of your project, brand, or work, then toss it overboard.

Making such tough, necessary choices isn't easy. You'll feel guilty; we certainly have. But keep the end goal in mind. You're here to do and be the best, and hanging on to an idea, product, service—or person—that isn't working and trying to salvage it just wastes energy and resources.

When it comes to your work, learn to let some things go. Early in our careers we made the mistake of becoming infatuated with a design solution or an idea for a client. Even if the client wasn't feeling it, we clung to it like a desperate ex. We still fight for what we believe in, but we've also learned to keep a rational distance so we can cast aside what isn't working and move on more quickly.

When Apple engineers presented Steve Jobs with a prototype of the first iPod, he told them it was too big. They protested that it was impossible to make it smaller. So Jobs dropped it in an aquarium. Bubbles floated to the top of the water and he said, "Those are air bubbles. That means there's space in there. Make it smaller."

As frustrating as it can be, you reserve the right to go back to square one if you can make something better. Of course, you'll make people angry when you do this. Some will feel betrayed; others will jump ship. Not everyone will understand the ruthless sacrifices that are necessary to turn a big vision into a reality. Don't let their negative energy drain yours. Make the call and get the ship moving again. Every choice must serve a purpose.

So how do you find the horses that might need to be sacrificed? Ask yourself these questions:

- "What am I holding on to for my ego or for selfish reasons?"
- "What product or service sells well but doesn't serve the vision?"

- → "What wastes my time, hurts my energy, or distracts from my vision?"
- → "Who on my team isn't pushing us forward?"

If you want to adult the hell out of this, take the final step and make a "hit list." List all the things that you care deeply about. Assign each one a number that designates how willing you'd be to throw that thing into the sea for the greater good.

1: Yes, I'll toss it. This is something easily disposable.

2: Tough call, maybe? This means the choice is a real bitch.

3: Hell no! This one's ride or die.

Now go back and take a long, hard look at each. This will help you see what you can do with and without, what you're really willing to sacrifice, and what's completely off the table. Often, what gets you here, won't get you there.

9

BE A HEADLIGHT

In 1963, in the "Letter from Birmingham Jail," Martin Luther King Jr. criticized the religious community for "standing as a tail-light behind other community agencies rather than a headlight leading men to higher levels of justice." He recognized that the world needs more of us to be headlights that illuminate the way forward. Most people don't make it their responsibility to provide a better life for others, but Rare Breeds do. Headlights expose things hidden by darkness so that we can move in a direction that is good, right, and true. Audacious Rare Breeds use their bold spirit to help others find their way.

This is different from "Do What Can't Be Done" because it is more about doing what *should* be done. It's about doing something groundbreaking for someone else, not yourself. So many people are just trying to make it in environments that lack the resources and opportunities they need to succeed.

When you're a headlight, you take actions that inspire others to find the Rare Breed within themselves.

› Light the Way

Dallas chef Chad Houser wanted to be a headlight before he even understood what that meant. He might have had a conventional restaurant career had he not taken the chance to teach eight young men in a Dallas County juvenile detention facility how to make ice cream for a competition at a local farmer's market. Surprisingly, one of his students beat contestants from high-end college culinary programs and took home the trophy. Houser recalls, "He said to me, 'I just love to cook, make food, give it to people, and put a smile on their face.'"

Houser was disturbed by the reality facing that enthusiastic young chef: crime, segregation, abuse, poverty, drug use, mental illness, lack of opportunity. So he resolved to do something about it with the only tool he knew: food. He came up with an audacious idea to open a nonprofit restaurant that would hire at-risk youth coming out of the juvenile justice system and train them as culinary professionals.

Naturally, the professional dream crushers (who have a chapter in *every* city) told him he was a fool for thinking he could take "throwaway" teens out of jail, teach them to play with knives and fire, and run a successful restaurant with this business model. Investors said things like *They'll stab each other in the kitchen!* and *Those kids don't want to work, they just want a check!* Houser didn't listen, and in 2015, after proving out the concept with a series of highly successful pop-up restaurants, he opened Café Momentum in Dallas. The gourmet restaurant provides a transformative experience through a twelve-month, post-release paid internship program for young men and women coming out of juvenile detention. Interns rotate through all aspects of the restaurant, focusing on life and social skills, coaching, and development to help them achieve their greatest potential.

Houser was named one of *Good* magazine's "Good 100" at the cutting edge of creative impact across the globe. In 2017, he won the $50,000 top prize from the BBVA Momentum program for social entrepreneurs. And in 2018, CNN added him to its roster of CNN Heroes. Houser emphasizes that that kind of recognition is more about the kids he helps than about him. "Receiving such an accolade is not necessarily validating for me, but for the kids," he says. "They show up every day, they trust a guy they have no reason to trust, and they keep showing up amidst horrible odds and life situations."

Houser could have continued living his life for himself, becoming a famous chef and making bold professional moves for the sake of his own legacy. But he chose a different path—one that enlightens others to the conditions of the marginalized and changes stigmas. That's what headlights do.

› How to Own This Mantra

Is it just us, or do you feel inadequate now, too? We're sort of kidding, but we know what Chad Houser would say to that: just go *do something*. It's damn good advice, because so much of making an impact is simply *starting*.

What really makes this Mantra powerful is that you're not just dragging people along in your wake; you're helping them find *their* passion or *their* courage to become Rare Breeds themselves. Eighty-five percent of the kids who pass through Café Momentum's program have not wound up back in the juvenile justice system during that critical year after getting out. That's huge because the overall recidivism rate in Texas is more than 40 percent. By breaking the cycle of a life spent in and out of jail, who knows how many of Café Momentum's interns will go on to change their communities, own their own businesses, or pass it forward on an even larger scale? We'll bet a really proud number.

Here are a few things to chew on:

KNOW WHERE TO SHINE YOUR LIGHT. Success expert Richard St. John suggests, "First think wide, then focus." Problem solving requires taking tons of information in, processing that information, and finally focusing on what matters. Razor-sharp focus will allow you to zero in and find answers. Where is there a problem or social issue that you can illuminate? How will you expose it? Where are the inefficient markets, underserved people, too-high prices, or damaged environments? What can you fix, and who can you help? Knowing where to focus your efforts is critical to successful outcomes.

MATCH YOUR SKILLS TO THE PROBLEM. Houser is a chef, so he decided to open a restaurant. You may be an engineer, a designer, a law student, a musician, a builder. How can you apply your talents to shine a positive light on the issues you care about?

BUILD YOUR PLATFORM. Find opportunities to share what you know. Houser speaks around the country about the *reason* Café Momentum exists and the incredible work it does. It's not for the money, it's not for the recognition. It's to help a group of people who have been dismissed, underestimated, and forgotten. And that's what drives thousands of people each year to the award-winning restaurant. In giving his cause a platform, he's lifting others.

PUT YOUR WHEELS IN MOTION. There are great organizations that offer volunteering for a day, week, or month so you can jump in and start serving others. Check out groups like DoSomething.org, Points of Light, and VolunteerMatch.

Mahatma Gandhi said, "In the midst of darkness, light persists." It's a reminder to be a headlight in a world of taillights.

10

HAVE AN UNUSUAL DREAM

> "But I don't want to go among mad people," Alice remarked.
> "Oh, you can't help that," said the Cat: "we're all mad here. I'm mad. You're mad."
> "How do you know I'm mad?" said Alice.
> "You must be," said the Cat, "or you wouldn't have come here."
>
> **—Lewis Carroll, *Alice's Adventures in Wonderland***

In his poem "Andrea del Sarto," Robert Browning wrote, "Ah, but a man's reach should exceed his grasp, / Or what's a heaven for?" In other words, to do great things, we should aspire to what appears illogical and unachievable; we should have the overconfidence to dream and chase the absurd.

From Leonardo da Vinci to Nikola Tesla, we've always loved the unusual dreamers. We love that they make us feel like kids at a carnival, where anything is possible and people can travel to the stars. That's why we cheer when SpaceX lands two of its Falcon Heavy first-stage rocket boosters back on the pad at Cape Canaveral. In a world that tries to bully us into coloring inside the lines, we can use our audacity to push something so far into the void, we pull back miracles.

› Success Sucks, Literally

Sir James Dyson had an unusual dream back in 1979: to engineer the world's best vacuum cleaner, one that would never clog or lose suction. It's not like there was anything terribly wrong with the vacuums of the time; they worked just fine. Vacuums weren't broken. But Sir James couldn't stand the idea that the technology was far short of what it could be, so he set out to make it better and more beautiful.

What makes Dyson a Rare Breed is that he didn't care that there wasn't any urgency in what he was doing. He didn't care that he was going up against giant companies like Hoover and Electrolux. He listened to his gut, leveraged his audacious spirit, and built more than five thousand failed prototypes before he finally got his central system—a cyclonic separator inspired by the gear at a sawmill—to work. Then it took years more to get the first Dyson vacuum into stores, during which he and his wife nearly lost everything. Despite those early struggles, nothing stopped him from not only bringing his vision to life but making it a commercial success.

Today, the name Dyson is not only synonymous with vacuum cleaners but with engineering flair that routinely challenges and reimagines commonplace products. Not a fan (pun intended) of traditional room fans? Try the Air Multiplier, a fan without blades. That thing will blow your face off. Don't like old-fashioned wheelbarrows that wobble? No problem, here's one that rides on a giant ball. Tired of the time it takes to dry your hair with a clunky hair dryer? Meet the Supersonic, the most innovative, futuristic hair tool (and the most awarded hair dryer) you've ever seen. We could go on for a while; Dyson is constantly testing and innovating (next up, electric cars).

The point is, Sir James doesn't believe in settling for *just fine*. He's not interested in what gets the job done. He looks for ways to dream up slick designs that work better than their *just fine* counterparts, taking on whole industries with a vested interest in blowing the doors off mediocrity. The riskier the idea, the harder he pushes to make his unusual ideas a reality.

You could say the same about NBA superstar LeBron James, who strode into a new world of entrepreneurship and philanthropy when he opened the I Promise School in his hometown of Akron, Ohio. The inaugural class of 240 third- and fourth-graders enjoyed free bikes and helmets, food for families, job placement for parents, and more. Yes, it's a great example of giving back to the community that raised you, but it's more than that. It's *trailblazing*. A new model for private-public education led by a basketball player? Why not?

For big dreamers who trust the velocity of their dreams, nothing is off-limits.

> How to Own This Mantra

Dyson is an engineer, and he dreams like one, always deconstructing the inner workings of things and asking, "How can I design this better?" And then—and this is the important part—he acts on that big bizarre dream. That's the mindset you'll need if you want to start bringing your Rare Breed audacity to this Mantra.

Having an unusual dream means more than caring about better gas mileage or a faster microchip; it means being not only *willing* but *eager* to take on other players in an arena. Every ounce of you must outdo and outdream them.

Here are a few ideas:

GET UNCOMFORTABLE. In a short video, Rabbi Abraham Twerski explains how lobsters grow, relating that growth to personal development. In order to get bigger, a lobster must throw off its confining, protective shell numerous times during its life and produce a larger one. "The stimulus for a lobster to be able to grow is that it feels uncomfortable," Twerski explains. Comfortable people don't grow and therefore build boring companies and brands. Rare Breeds throw off the uncomfortable and build unusual companies and brands.

LEARN EVERYTHING ABOUT AREAS THAT FASCINATE YOU. Want to make next-gen cars? Learn about antique cars and spaceships. Aching to bring the internet of things to small urban farmers? Try volunteering on a farm for a summer, learning firsthand how crops are grown, harvested, and brought to market. Read, watch videos, attend conferences, feed your mind and your dreams. Take things apart to see how they work and then put them back together *differently*.

LOOK FOR THE SEAMS. A seam can be defined as a vulnerable area—a place in an industry, category, or economy where there's a weak spot—an unmet need or widespread dissatisfaction. Dyson found that everybody hated the hand dryers commonly found in restrooms. Rather than shrug and say, "Yeah, but they work *just fine*," he completely reimagined the category and dreamed up the Airblade. By designing something that dried hands faster and more thoroughly, he created opportunity out of dissatisfaction. That's finding and exploiting a seam.

There are a thousand ways to out-brand, out-innovate, and out-execute your competition. But first, you've got to have an unusual dream. Now, go invent a transporter already.

11

SEE YOURSELF FROM ORBIT

Imagine floating in zero gravity, untethered from the pale blue dot we call home. As you free-fall around Earth, your perspective shifts. You experience total wonder and awe. The world you thought you knew is gone, and in its place is a single blue-white sphere, fragile and beautiful. You can't see national borders or lines of latitude and longitude. You can, however, see the great river systems, the deserts, the ice caps, the boreal forests, the lights of the cities. You see it unified, one people striving to survive, bigger than division and politics.

Just like that, you're transformed. With a view you never imagined, you see patterns and connections that you never realized were there. You will never look at humanity, the earth, or the human condition the same way again.

› The Overview Effect

This sounds dramatic, but it's actually something called the *overview effect*. It's a profound cognitive shift that some astronauts have reported when they view the earth from space. The sight of our planet from space, a delicate envelope of water and air supporting all life, changes them to their core. They return home humbled, talking about unity, protecting our planetary home, and ending war and conflict. It's a kind of cosmic euphoria that makes the experiencer suddenly, exquisitely aware of his or her place in the universe.

In a short film by Planetary Collective called *Overview*, David Beaver, cofounder of the Overview Institute, recounts the sentiments from one of the astronauts on the Apollo 8 mission: "When we originally went to the moon, our total focus was on the moon. We weren't thinking about looking back at the earth. But now that we've done it, that may well have been the most important reason we went."

Apollo 14 astronaut Edgar Mitchell was probably the most vocal person to experience the overview effect. While walking on the moon's surface in 1971, he found himself aware of the connectedness between every atom and molecule in the cosmos, and understood that every person, creature, and object on Earth was a part of that sacred whole. "From out there on the moon, international politics look so petty," he said. "You want to grab a politician by the scruff of the neck and drag him a quarter of a million miles out and say, 'Look at that, you son of a bitch.'"

Caught up in the bustle of being your bad, bold self, it's easy to lose perspective and fall into the traps that your audacity places out for you. You get a little cocky. You pushed an idea at work for the sake of it without making sure it was the right one. You published an editorial just for the shock value only to realize you got some facts wrong. Egg, meet face.

Stepping back and seeing the big picture is an epic wake-up call and can be a huge turning point. It puts everything into perspective, changing how you think and how you do things. You start to see how you fit in the larger whole, and from there you can leverage your perspective for progress instead of peacocking. That self-awareness is powerful.

› How to Own This Mantra

When was the last time you stepped back and looked at your business, your brand, your work, or your *life* from a bird's-eye view? If it's been awhile (or never), we highly recommend you take the time to do some expansive thinking. What you see, and what you *sense*, could change everything.

There are some tried-and-true tricks for getting this renewed perspective. You need to first stop focusing on the trivial BS and the chaotic happenings of the every day. Instead of wasting your time playing "name that city" (when you're not puking from space sickness, of course), stop messing around and really *look* at the big picture.

Try this zooming-out meditation: First, sit down, close your eyes, and zoom in. See yourself inside the room; notice the things next to you, the windows, the doors. Sense the whole space. Then begin to zoom out, taking your awareness beyond the boundaries of the room or house. See the birds, cars, people. Expand your awareness to the city. What would it look like from a hot-air balloon? Keep zooming out to see the entire region from a plane just below the cloud line, and then even farther to see the topography of the whole globe, the outline of all the countries. Now see the world and all its wonders from space. It's glorious, isn't it?

Now that you're zoomed out, imagine where you want to be in five, ten, or twenty years. Look hard at whether you're doing the things that will get you to that goal.

Also, ask someone close to you to describe your journey from their point of view. Tell them to be honest about roads you should have taken or mistakes you've made. It's easy to become so focused on the bends in the road that you lose sight of where you're going. You're not looking for advice here, but perspective.

Seeing yourself from orbit and reflecting on it all comes down to being self-aware—to have the ability to zoom out from yourself and see the bigger picture. Are you fractured? Or whole? Have you made too many compromises? Have you passed on opportunities because you were afraid or because you were too comfortable? Have you failed to maintain relationships that might have helped you? Did you have a bigger vision for your life that's gotten stuffed into an old trunk because of the demands of the day to day?

Answer some tough questions, and be honest with yourself:

- → Am I where I thought I'd be five years ago?
- → If not, why? What went wrong?
- → What am I blind to?
- → What mistakes have I kept repeating and how can I break the cycle?
- → Who's encouraging me and who's holding me back?
- → Am I even happy?

Maybe you're burned out. Maybe the long hours and demands are threatening to wreck your relationships. Or maybe you've just made enough compromises and taken enough shortcuts that you're leaving your extraordinary potential on the table. The only way to know that is to zoom out.

Perspective is everything.

12

BURN THE PLAN

> We must be willing to get rid of the life we've planned, so as to have the life that is waiting for us.
>
> **—Joseph Campbell, from *Reflections on the Art of Living: A Joseph Campbell Companion***

On April 4, 2013, armed with a desire to see our business grow, the two of us packed some bags, our laptops, and a roll of duct tape and set out for a two-week road trip. We were headed to New Orleans for a business conference. Sounds pretty normal, right? (Except for the duct tape; more on that later.)

We had no idea we wouldn't be home until Christmas.

Hitting up New Orleans was like getting seduced. We stayed in NOLA for two weeks—and instead of heading home, we went west. From roadside diners to Helldorado Days in Tombstone, Arizona, dropping in on Willie Nelson's favorite music joint in Luckenbach, Texas, to a dude ranch, we roamed from town to town getting tips for our next location from the people we met along the way. We drove through Louisiana swamps, Texas Hill Country, deserts, giant white sand hills, and up the California coast. Somewhere in Houston, Sunny backed out of a garage and tore the driver's side mirror off the

SUV. The neon duct tape we'd tossed in the back came in mighty handy . . . until we were driving through New Mexico, when the tape melted and the mirror fell off.

Along the way, we shared our story and built our social media audience, too.

We didn't have a plan. We lived in the moment. We chose to experience what life was sending our way in real time. It wasn't comfortable sleeping in the car some nights, but when you're stranded in the desert with nothing but stars above you, the sacrifice is worth the chance of experiencing life in raw, piercingly beautiful new ways. We've never been happier, more productive, more focused, more creative—or more *alive.* And when we went home, we had an arsenal of new clients to boot. None of that would've happened had we stuck to the plan.

› A Goal Is a Dream with a . . .

From mentors to self-help books to celebrities, everybody says it: to reach a goal, you need to have a concrete plan, create action items, look before you leap, and . . . oh my God, are you as bored with this as we are? Having a plan can be limiting and even useless when it comes to achieving goals, because it boxes you in. So when you're naturally daring, you need to give yourself permission to kick the plan to the curb.

Over the years, we've been able to thrive without a plan.

- → We built a multimillion-dollar business without a plan.
- → We traveled cross-country for nine months without a plan.
- → We moved to different cities without a plan.
- → We secured a six-figure book deal and then rejected it for a different publisher. *Not part of the plan.*

The worst part about a plan is that it can make you resistant to change. The unknown is scary, so you make a plan to confront a future you're guessing at. The plan becomes a psychologically soothing security blanket. You're a slave to it. When your eyes are glued to the plan you've drawn for yourself, you miss all the awesome experiences that happen off the beaten path. When you start to believe that reality is *obligated* to proceed according to your plan, you're in trouble. Because it won't. Things happen, people drop the ball, luck runs out, the world changes, *you* change. If you cling to the plan like it's a lucky rabbit's foot, you'll likely panic and give up. Ponder this:

Sometimes, burning the plan is the best plan of all.

Being free of a predetermined outcome keeps you open to the kind of spontaneity that leads to unforgettable relationships, experiences, and opportunities you might otherwise overlook. You learn to place bets, make uncomfortable choices, and say "I'm in."

› Doers not Planners

Cortney and Robert Novogratz are a husband-and-wife, self-taught design and architecture powerhouse who seem to excel at everything. They've created wildly original spaces for living, working, and playing for more than twenty-five years, including redesigning what seems like half of New York City and renovating the Hollywood Hills castle where they used to live with their seven children (yes, you read that right).

They have books, their own retail brand, past shows on Bravo and HGTV, and a gypsy-like life. But how? We can barely manage to get our work done, feed the office dog, and water the plants before crashing in the clothes we wore all day. How does this couple basically run the world while living a life that looks like the subject of a feature in *Envy the Fuck Out of Us* magazine?

The answer isn't as complicated as you might expect. The Novogratz (as they call themselves) take giant leaps and have crazy vision. Full stop. That vision—not branding initiatives or financial projections—guides their lives. In fact, they never planned to be designers. When they bought their first home, they rented out every room to close friends, who helped them finish remodeling the building on a shoestring budget. They kept buying buildings in Soho and turning them into showpieces. Eventually, musician Suzanne Vega rented from them, and the press came calling. They decided they had a knack for developing properties, so they founded their company, 6 Design. The fly-by-the-seat-of-your-pants model never changed.

No life maps. No 150-page business plans. The Novogratz do what turns them on and run with it until it takes them somewhere. If they fall, they do their best to land on their feet. "People never tell you to jump off the highest bridge without a net but that's just what we do," they said in a 2015 *Forbes* interview. "The key is to be able to bounce when you hit the ground because it's never a straight line to the top. It's about fortitude, balls and believing in yourself when no one else will." That, perhaps more than their eye for design or business acumen, is the Novogratz's audacity.

› How to Own This Mantra

The Novogratz had the guts to say "burn the plan." They're doers, not planners. That is how they measure success—not checking off boxes on a list—and it is great advice when you're aiming for a life filled with adventure.

You might not think that's the smart path for an entrepreneur, but it often is. Business is risky, and taking that first step can be terrifying. Most people plan, plan, and plan some more. But they're just delaying out of fear. This is where your audacious side has the advantage.

If you're an independent professional, you're even more perfectly positioned to set fire to the idea of planning. You're already agile and versatile, working when and where you please. Why not relocate where the most lucrative work is and couch surf until you make it? Or buy a vintage trailer, turn it into a mobile design/writing/photography/whatever studio, and hit the road with a hashtag and a docuseries in your heart, turning yourself into an internet celeb? You can do it. It doesn't always require a hard-and-fast blueprint.

There are times when you'll need a plan in the short term. If you're raising funds for your business, you'll need to show investors a business plan. When you have a project with a tight deadline, you'll need a plan for everyone on your team to follow so the work gets done on time. That kind of planning is necessary.

But working and living without a plan is an adventure, and audacious Rare Breeds thrive on adventure (hello New Orleans! We miss you!). Building a thriving career from the ground up demands energy and joie de vivre. You don't get that from a boring, plodding plan. You get it when you're on the edge, figuring out what you truly love, experimenting with a broad range of new experiences that would normally make you hesitate, feeling brave and jittery with excitement, not knowing what's going to happen tomorrow.

Play the game, not the game plan.

VIRTUE 3

OBSESSED

Perfectionist. Relentless. Uncompromising. Neurotic. Fanatical.

An asset when your obsession propels you and others to exceed presumed limits, go the extra mile, uncover the flaws in ideas, and execute greatness.

A weakness when the demand for perfection leads to extreme overwork, stress, isolation, and insanity and paralyzes everyone with the terror of pressure and high expectations.

In observing that talent is a cheap commodity, author Stephen King compared it to a dull knife. While some people are born with big knives, he said, nobody is born with a sharp knife. What sharpens the knife, turning talent into genius, is "discipline and constant work." Being intelligent or gifted or having a big idea won't bring greatness in any field without a ridiculous, all-consuming, obsessive work ethic.

If you look at seminal figures throughout history, you see that obsession comes with the territory of genius. Think of Jack Kerouac typing the first draft of his masterpiece *On the Road* in a three-week frenzy (as legend has it) on one 120-foot scroll of paper.

Or Prince, so determined to make his live shows perfect that he often ran a three-hour sound check. Then he'd play a four-hour concert, load the band into a truck, and play a local club until 4 a.m. And then go to a studio at sunrise to work on new ideas.

Obsession submerges us beneath the warm waters of what psychologist Mihaly Csikszentmihalyi calls *flow*, that quasi-magical state of unbroken mental focus, and makes it okay to surrender to the current. Consequences come later, but while we're caught in that riptide of revising and inventing, we're all in.

Obsession is a secret ingredient in greatness because it makes us crazy enough to disregard rational limits. Whatever we want from life is only worth what we're willing to pay for it, and obsession makes everything—family, friends, romances, a social life, our time, even our health—negotiable. When success quotes us its price, obsession hands it a blank check and says, "Fill in the amount, I *must* get back to work." It's the ticket that gets us past the bouncer and into the club where names like Zuckerberg, Bezos, and Branson have held court before us.

I've gone seventy-nine hours without sleep, creating. When that flow is going, it's almost like a high. You don't want it

> to stop. You don't want to go to sleep for fear of missing something.
>
> —Dr. Dre

› Welcome to Club Obsessive

If you've contracted the obsessive bug, you know it. Every space you inhabit—room, desk, car—is littered with papers scrawled with designs, equations, and epiphanies, the debris left by the receding waters of your brainstorms. You kangaroo out of bed at 2 a.m. because ideas wind your brain up to methamphetamine speed. You iterate until your fingers bleed and your eyes burn, and you actually sketch out supply-chain diagrams or decision trees with a Sharpie on the walls of your shower.

You've never seen a final draft you couldn't revise in a compulsive quest for the just-so word. (If that word doesn't exist, you'll coin it.) Your capacity to freak and fret over the tiniest details leaves people red-faced with frustration—that is, until they're singing your praises for the tweak that made the whole thing shine. Your work never stops screaming at you from inside your skull, and matching it to your fever pitch of perfect makes you lose track of days, live on Kit Kats and Red Bull, and neglect your own well-being until your friends and family consider a dental floss, soap, and hot water intervention. And after you've restrained yourself from a wild-eyed lunge ("Just one last change!") as your work goes out the door, you sit back, spent and shaking, and vow, "I'm never doing this again."

But then you do. Over and over.

Sound familiar? You're in the club.

Now, stop apologizing for it. Being obsessive is often labeled as a vice because it can make you neglect all the other stakeholders in your life. People tell you to spend less time on your computer or at the office, but what else would you rather be doing besides creating your destiny one drop of sweat at a time? *Nothing*. For obsessed entrepreneurs and innovators, taking a break or a day off is pure torture. We *know*. We've skipped graduations and birthdays, declined wedding invites, and missed Ashleigh's own goddaughter's christening. We weren't always proud of those choices, but our obsessive natures prevailed.

› Meet Marie

From Leonardo da Vinci to James Madison to Amelia Earhart, the greats of the past were driven by compulsions to do the extraordinary and blessed with being exceptional doers. Exhibit A: Marie Curie, the only woman for whom an element on the Periodic Table is named. Yep, from Einsteinium to Rutherfordium, the rest of the table is a total sausage fest.

That matters, because when the former Maria Sklodowska was born in Warsaw in 1867, women were mostly ornaments and baby-makers who were forbidden from enrolling in Poland's finest universities. Maria had two battlements to storm: the gender bias of her time and the *tiny* matter of making pioneering scientific discoveries. She did both with such brilliance, style, and obsessive zeal that we're writing about her here.

Yes, Curie was brilliant. But she also had a fanatical drive. It wasn't uncommon for her to work in her lab until she collapsed from exhaustion. She labored for four years in an old shed to isolate a new element, radium, and continued even after it became clear that it was poisoning her. That drive, which ultimately killed her, also made her a pioneer in radioactivity research and earned her two Nobel prizes.

Curie once said, "I was taught that the way of progress was neither swift nor easy." She knew that greatness on her terms came at a price, and she never hesitated to cover that cost.

> It's the addicts that stay with it. They're not necessarily the most talented, they're just the ones that can't get it out of their systems.
>
> —Harold Brown

› The "Good Enough" Antidote

When you're a perfectionist, you'll attract some good-enoughers who will give annoying advice that's pretty predictable:

- "Jeez, lighten up, it's fine the way it is."
- "You're taking this way too seriously."
- "Nobody else is going to care like you do."
- "Step away and let someone else do it."
- "It's good enough to ship!"

Did just reading that list give you the heebie-jeebies? Obsessive folks particularly go bananas over that last one—"It's good enough to ship!" As brand consultants, when we hear that, we know its game over. The road to mediocrity becomes a downhill run. Instead of shaking things up, you're settling and hoping nobody catches on. You become BlackBerry. Worse, fraudster Theranos.

We work daily with companies where the leadership is veering dangerously close to swerving down Good Enough Avenue. When that happens, two things are inevitable. First, the team gets comfortable. Work past five? *Yeah, once in a while.* Did the customer okay it? *Then it's fine.* Change the world? *Nah, but we made our Q3 numbers.* If talent is a knife, comfort is a concrete block that blunts its edge until it can't cut anything.

Second, all the gifted people—the wild-eyed poets and tech tinkerers who signed on to actually *do something*—head for the exits. They move on to daring startups and passion projects where they can build what can't be built and do the impossible.

For obsessive Rare Breeds, there is no good enough. There's only "perfect" or "this sucks and I'm a complete failure." They can't stop or rest until good becomes great and great becomes unprecedented. That's certainly true for Es Devlin, a highly sought-after set designer. She's created stunning visuals for Adele, Lady Gaga, Katy Perry, and U2, among others. She put Kanye on top of a mountain that transformed into a volcano. She had Adele tour the world in front of seventy-four-foot screen projections of her own eyes; and she sent Miley Cyrus down a bubblegum-pink tongue-shaped fiberglass slide. And yet, she admits, "I can't actually think of a day when I haven't felt like I'm failing. I'm very, very rarely satisfied with anything that I make."

We spoke to chef Gavin Kaysen, owner of Spoon and Stable in Minneapolis and Bellecour in Wayzata, for our Rare Breed content series, and he told us that he once spent forty-five minutes discussing the preparation of one piece of asparagus. *One piece of asparagus that would be eaten in three seconds.* Contrast that to the chef who's fine with serving you lukewarm chicken in canned sauce. Sure, it's easier to shove food through the window than to agonize over every ingredient, but guess who's the one winning the James Beard Award?

We know all this because we're obsessed, too. One time, we spent three days in a row at the office because we couldn't stop fine-tuning a client's brand strategy to meet the deadline (hey, we Febrezed). We recorded the opening to our Rare Breed video series for *eleven* hours straight until our producer unplugged us by "accidentally" tripping over our sound equipment. Then there was that time we ran out of gas and left our car on the side of the road, running through dandelions in one-hundred-degree heat like two psychos to deliver a presentation on time.

Yes, obsession can drive you mad. You didn't drive away from college with visions of waking up on a conference room table covered in dry erase marker, with a pizza box for a pillow and ten angry breakup texts. You had a vision of starting something important. But suffering the slings and arrows of obsession is the toll you pay on the highway to big things.

It's a blessing and a curse to be obsessed. You execute with precision. You never overlook anything. And you're proud of everything you do—as you should be. But damn is it dangerous.

> The Dark Side of Obsession

Trouble starts when you refuse to recognize and respect your limits. History is bursting with cautionary tales of people who achieved wealth or immortality at the cost of things like their health or family or relationships. Charles Lindbergh barely saw his kids. Warren Buffet locked himself in a room reading financial reports while his wife entertained guests at their home. Catherine the Great worked fourteen hours a day and rarely ate. Poet Sylvia Plath's signature works, *Daddy* and *The Bell Jar*, are fraught with despair. Her obsession with death and the plague of her own self-doubt beg the question: Could she have created such seminal works without all those demons? She developed a habit of fearing she'd lost her talent, leading to stress and depression. Then she would bounce back on the strength of her brilliance. That's a repetitive and vicious cycle common among obsessive geniuses, and it ended with her sticking her head in an oven at age thirty. Obsession without guardrails becomes a force for self-destruction. The intensity that makes mediocrity a four-letter word can also consume your life. You know this. As an obsessed person, you can be fastidious, inflexible, overly critical. You have a hard time trusting and delegating to anyone else. You override others. You have to put your stamp on every decision. Mistakes are mortal sins. If there's a scuff on the finish or a line of code out of place, you'll spot it before anyone else has time to get out a magnifying glass. Obsessives are hypervigilant. Your thoughts scurry around like millions of ants on a mound of sugar. *You let nothing go.*

Film director Stanley Kubrick is a cautionary tale and poster child for obsessives. Few people have ever matched his awesome, paranoid, and crushing perfectionism. He produced masterpieces that ranged from *Dr. Strangelove* to *2001: A Space Odyssey* and *Full Metal Jacket*, but he put himself and everyone around him through hell to do it. Kubrick insisted on controlling every aspect of his work, from casting and screenwriting to editing, lighting, and music. He drove studios crazy by sometimes taking years to edit a film, searching for a cut that might not even exist among the footage he had shot.

His attention to detail bordered on the maddening and absurd, such as the time during an all-night shoot of the crucifixion scene for *Spartacus* when he was unhappy with the look of the extra on the—and we are not making this up—twentieth cross from the left. Kubrick told his assistant director, Marshall Green, to walk out and tell the guy on the cross to move more. Green, long since sick of the director's shit, trudged out to the cross, then came back and said, "It's a fucking dummy." Kubrick famously replied, "Then put on wires and wiggle it."

But Kubrick's teeth-gnashing perfectionism was most infamous in his obsession with running his actors through endless takes of the same scene to the point where some threatened to quit. For example, he once made Tom Cruise walk through a door ninety-seven times during the filming of *Eyes Wide Shut.*

That's the duality of this Virtue. It can be the rite of passage to worldly success, but it can also paralyze. Extreme obsession crushes momentum, leads to irrational decision-making and flawed business logic, and compels endless iteration that never produces a thing. It breeds resentment in others and wrecks mental and physical well-being. The key is to know which side of obsessiveness you're channeling and stay firmly on the right side of the line, out of the path of oncoming traffic. You must not turn down your gift for perfection but rather corral it so it is constructive instead of destructive.

> There's no way I can stop writing, it's a form of insanity.
>
> —**Charles Bukowski, *Women***

› Obsession = Perfectionism + Purpose + Love

Healthy, productive obsession isn't just about pulling espresso-powered all-nighters perfecting your business plan or revising your product design until your eyeballs start to quiver. It's about doing those things in the service of something that's wormed its way inside you and won't leave. Being madly in love with your mission, infecting the people you're leading with that same love, and doing it all for a purpose that's bigger than making money—these things let you pay the crushing bill your obsession lays on you.

Ayah Bdeir knows this. She's founder and CEO of littleBits, which creates open-source electronic modules that let anyone play with robotics, engineering, and design. Growing up in Beirut, she was obsessed with tinkering and taking things apart to see how they worked. A designer and engineer, she first discovered her obsessive zeal for both when she was a kid and her father brought home software for making greeting cards. Bdeir became consumed by the software and spent hours designing cards, banners that she printed on the family's dot-matrix printer, and anything else she could create. It was her first look at how design and creativity could take over her mind.

A stint at MIT showed her that the ability to design and build things that solve problems in the real world had the power to capture people's imaginations. Since then, Bdeir has raised $60 million and taken littleBits global, but growing the company never stops being a punishing experience. What keeps her going is her obsession with her purpose.

"Entrepreneurship is now glamorous and sexy, but it's very difficult," she says in a 2016 *Wired* interview. "Unless you are obsessed by a problem, then you should not start a company. . . . What lifts you up is the mission, seeing the impact of what you're doing. Unless you feel in your blood that what you're creating needs to exist, you will not have enough fuel to take you through."

Why do obsessives often appear to be listening to an inner voice that only they can hear? Because they *are.* For those of us who are obsessive, results are secondary to our belief that there's a right way to create something—a physics in which the position of every atom matters and the placement of a syllable is the difference between burning a message into the audience's brain and leaving it flopping by the side of the road. We just have to do it that way. We can't let it go. We can't say it's fine, lock the door behind us, and go have a beer. Imperfection sits on us like a mosquito bite, itching furiously, until we have to scratch it.

While you're scratching, consider the following four tools for making the most of the Mantras that follow:

1. BE IN LOVE WITH YOUR OBSESSION.

It's love when no price seems too high—when Sisyphean effort and nocturnality that would embarrass Dracula make you shrug. When it's love, you'll pay the price, dust yourself off, and then do it all over again.

2. CHASE AWAY EVERYBODY WHO'S NOT AS OBSESSED AS YOU.

The compulsive push for better and more is a great way to separate those who share your mission from those who just want a paycheck. Not everybody will be willing to pay the price you ask them to pay. That's fine. The ones who survive will make you great, and vice versa.

3. KNOW HOW FAR IS TOO FAR.

You can't rely on your significant other to pull you back when you haven't slept for forty-eight hours or you're snarling at everyone in sight. Is your obsession creating clarity, focus, and purpose? Or is it blinding you from your own self-destruction? Know your limits and understand when it's time to shut it down and step away.

4. SET THE STANDARD OF EXCELLENCE.

You'll always be judged by the quality, originality, and innovation of your work. Your standards must be top notch. If a piece of your work isn't coming together, it's up to you to try to get it to the level where it should be. You need to define for yourself and for others the standards of excellence you will always expect.

As you read the Mantras and question the work that threatens to consume you, remember that obsession isn't a matter of choice. It's the way Rare Breeds are wired. It's the way *you're* wired. It's the engine that thrums and thunders under your hood, and you can't change it any more than you can change the color of your eyes. It's what you *do* with your obsession that matters. The people who surrender to their obsessive natures are the ones who finally throw up their hands and say, "Fine, you drive," and then climb into the shotgun seat, buckle up, and hang on as their obsession punches the accelerator and lays rubber on the road to marvels.

13

MASSAGE THE OCTOPUS

You probably know that the "ten thousand hours" rule of mastery—made famous by Malcolm Gladwell in his 2008 book *Outliers*—has been debunked by researchers, including Anders Ericsson, the psychologist who came up with the idea in the first place. According to Ericsson, practice *does* make a difference in developing aptitude; it just takes a lot more than ten thousand hours. He observed that classical musicians who win international competitions typically put in about *twenty-five thousand hours* of dedicated practice—or about three hours a day for twenty years. Furthermore, the type of practice that leads to mastery can't just be casual fooling around. It has to be, in Ericsson's words, "deliberate, dedicated time spent focusing on improvement."

You see the point. An obsession with being the best won't get you to the top without intense, focused, difficult, repetitive training. The kind of training that's tedious and backbreaking. The kind you come to hate.

Okay, but what the fuck does this have to do with massaging an octopus?

› A Little Lower and to the Left

Meet Jiro Ono, the ninety-three-year-old owner of Sukiyabashi Jiro, a tiny three-Michelin-starred sushi restaurant located in a Tokyo subway station. He's widely regarded as the finest sushi chef in the world. Hawaiian-born Barack Obama—who presumably ate a lot of sushi growing up—ate at Jiro's counter and told reporters, "That's some good sushi right there."

That's no accident. Jiro is renowned for three things: his lifelong obsession with the signature Japanese cuisine (the title of the wonderful documentary about him, *Jiro Dreams of Sushi*, was inspired by the fact that he invents sushi dishes in his sleep and awakens to write down his ideas), his innovative preparation methods, and his rigorous approach to training aspiring sushi *itamae*.

Jiro teaches apprentice chefs, who train for ten years under his leadership, how to perform tedious grunt work, including massaging raw octopus for forty-five minutes at a time for up to nine months. Get your mind out of the gutter; the octopus doesn't get a happy ending. Hand massage is the best way to make the notoriously tough meat perfectly tender for expectant guests.

Master the art of octopus massage and the apprentices *might* get to cook the rice. A few hundred hours of that and *maybe* they'll be asked to make the egg sushi. They'll think they've made egg sushi perfect enough to serve, only to see Jiro dump it into the trash. It took one apprentice two hundred tries before Jiro found his work acceptable enough to place before his customers.

Most apprentices throw in their *hachimaki*. Why? They can't stand the tedium. They want to skip to the end, to be a respected sushi chef, but not put in the work required to earn the title. It's frustrating to try your hand at something and not get a gold star right away.

But that's not how mastery works. Only the apprentices who can humble themselves and appreciate the beauty of learning can see the repetitive work for what it is: a process that primes them for greatness.

› Be a Student for Life

Perhaps you can hack a few things, but you miss out on the lesson. Which really is the point, isn't it? A lesson teaches us the true meaning of a craft. Once you understand the lesson, then you can move on to the next task. And then master that, and so on. That's why it's important to be a student for life. The more you fill your cart with lessons, the greater your knowledge of the world will be.

Most of us are terrible at this. We want a fast track to the top and often think we're better than we are. Somewhere along the line, we shift from student to know-it-all. We're unwilling to be schooled, taught, or surprised. We get closed-minded, feel defensive, and form inflexible ideas of the world around us. In doing so, we suffer.

In his 2012 book *Mastery*, Robert Greene observes that all the greatest masters have a development phase in their lives, a "largely self-directed apprenticeship" that lasts five to ten years and "receives little attention because it does not contain stories of great achievement or discovery." He goes on to say, "The goal of apprenticeship is not money, a good position, a title, or a diploma, but rather the transformation of your mind and character."

In a culture of demand and immediacy, overnight success is a myth. Rarely do you see the thousands of failed attempts, discouragement, missed bull's-eyes, punched walls, crying jags, and painful repetition all great masters endure.

As Jiro Ono says in *Jiro Dreams of Sushi*: "I do the same thing over and over again. Improving bit by bit. There is always a yearning to achieve more. I will continue to climb, trying to reach the top—but no one knows where the top is." Rare Breeds see themselves as always students, sometimes teachers, and rarely, if ever, masters.

› How to Own This Mantra

Mastery—the kind that has you massaging an octopus—is about more than putting in the hours. It's about personal transformation. Think about how a martial artist earns a black belt. It's not just about punches and kicks. Black belt practitioners must spend years developing discipline, self-control, fitness, and patience. That's why by the time students earn their coveted black belts, they aren't just more skilled. They're different people.

In Western culture, it's difficult for many to appreciate this way of thinking. Agonizing dedication is often seen as the enemy of productivity and, in some ways, unfruitful. Jiro Ono disagrees. "Once you have decided on your occupation you must immerse yourself in your work. You have to fall in love with your work," he says. "You must dedicate your life to mastering your skill. That's the secret of success and is the key to being regarded honorably."

In other words, learn to love massaging that fucking cephalopod.

Here are a few rules regarding mastery:

RULE 1: Whatever you want to be the best at, practice improving it every day.

RULE 2: Be more patient. Patience is rare.

RULE 3: Show up and stop complaining.

RULE 4: Find the lesson in everything and everyone.

RULE 5: Quit filling your time with distractions; fill it with chances to learn and grow.

RULE 6: Do it *all*. Don't just cook; wash dishes, wait tables, and manage the books, too.

RULE 7: Ask questions, even if you think they're stupid.

Sarah Lewis, author of the 2014 book *The Rise: Creativity, the Gift of Failure, and the Search for Mastery*, said it best: "Mastery is not merely a commitment to a goal, but to a curved-line, constant pursuit."

14

FIND YOUR 4 A.M.

While accepting the 2016 ESPY Icon Award, Kobe Bryant addressed his fellow athletes about the truth behind the greats: "We're not on this stage just because of talent or ability. We're up here because of 4 a.m. We're up here because of two-a-days or five-a-days. We're up here because we had a dream and let nothing stand in our way. If anything tried to bring us down, we used it to make us stronger."

Bryant is famous for his legendary work ethic—and his obsessive side. He once called his personal trainer at 3:30 in the morning to say he needed some help with his conditioning work. The trainer, roused from sleep, got dressed and headed to the gym and found Bryant already soaked in sweat, practicing on his own.

Another time, eager to add cycling to his training routine, Bryant had his trainer rent mountain bikes, and then they hit a Las Vegas trail and rode forty miles, not getting back until 2 a.m. By 7:30 that same morning, Bryant was in the gym working out.

This is typical Bryant: consistently outworking *everyone*.

Most people won't do what it takes to be truly excellent in their field, but then they feel frustrated and demoralized by not being where they want. They won't work weekends. They'd rather party than study. They live for Fridays. They wouldn't dare show up two hours early for work to get a head start on a project. And they sure as hell aren't rolling out in the middle of the night to shoot free throws.

But Rare Breeds are different. They work their asses off. They kill it in the gym when everyone else is sleeping. They study microbiology on their birthday. They practice guitar scales until their fingertips bleed. They burn the midnight oil, not just for a few days or weeks, but daily, and over a lifetime. And their diligence pays off.

One of the greatest female tennis players of all time, Serena Williams, is obsessed with excellence through effort. "Luck has nothing to do with it," she told ESPN, "because I have spent many, many hours, countless hours, on the court working for my one moment in time, not knowing when it would come."

Sure, it helps to have natural talent, but mindset and effort are what breed success. Just think about how many people you know who are ridiculously gifted, but lazy AF. Now think of someone who has a lot less talent but grinds his or her face off. Talent doesn't take you to the top. Hustle does.

› How to Own This Mantra

To achieve excellence in your field of endeavor, you need to think like a champion. You need to put in two-a-days and five-a-days. You need to give *effort* to achieve that excellence.

It all boils down to simply *deciding*. Deciding that it's intolerable that anyone could be superior to you in your field, whether that's writing code, playing the violin, mixing cocktails, or distance running.

Martin Luther King Jr. left us with this beautiful piece of advice from a 1967 sermon: "Even if it falls your lot to be a street sweeper, go on out and sweep streets like Michelangelo painted pictures; sweep streets like Handel and Beethoven composed music; sweep streets like Shakespeare wrote poetry; sweep streets so well that all the host of heaven and earth will have to pause and say, 'Here lived a great street sweeper who swept his job well.'"

Ask yourself:

- What am I going to be the best at?
- What routine or practice do I need to do every day?
- What material do I have to study?
- How can I heighten my productivity while I'm in the flow? Everyone in the profession is doing the same humdrum things to sharpen their skills, so what can I do that's *extra*?

Challenge yourself to improve. There are plenty of people out there who have as much ability as you do, and some who have more. You have no control over that. But you have complete control over how hard you'll work, when and how you'll work, and what you'll sacrifice to be the best.

15

SIGN YOUR WORK

When you hear "cardigan" you think of those studious little sweaters that button down the front. But the Cardigan we're talking about is a charming bayside town on the far western edge of Wales that once thrived as Britain's largest supplier of jeans. For almost forty years, thirty-five thousand pairs of jeans came out of Cardigan every week. But in 2001, the denim factories closed in pursuit of profits overseas. Hundreds of world-class jeans makers were without a job.

A decade later, David Hieatt, a social entrepreneur and founder of the Do Lectures, decided it was time for the town to make jeans again. In 2012, he opened the doors to Hiut Denim, a raw and selvedge denim company with a war cry to change the denim industry. Inside every pair of jeans is the handwritten signature of the person who made them.

For Hieatt, signing your work is part of his family's heritage. His father was an electrician in the merchant navy who quickly found out that most of the ship's electricians didn't really care about doing a good job. If a component failed, they usually blamed their shoddy work on the previous guy. That steamed David's dad; he was a perfectionist, and those "shirkers" drove him nuts. He was the kind of man who gave concentrated attention to every circuit, fuse, and wire, knowing that everything he did was a reflection of who he was. He inspected everything, assumed nothing, and if something could be done better, he did it.

Then one day, in a little bit of midcentury shade throwing, he started putting his initials—JBH—on every job he did. It was his way of telling the world that he was proud of his work, that *I did this!* It was also a way of setting himself apart from the slouches, even if it meant taking the heat for a mistake.

That sense of respect for the craft has found its way into Hiut Denim. Hieatt and his team obsess over every stitch, rivet, cut, and color. It's not the quick, cheap, or easy way to go about it, but they don't care about quick, cheap, and easy. They care about being the best at what they do.

› Your Work Is Your Reputation

There may not be anyone with higher standards than legendary Swiss watchmaker Philippe Dufour. Regarded by many as the finest craftsman of timepieces in the world, Dufour makes watches that watch enthusiasts and timepiece professionals around the globe lust after. Because he finishes each watch by hand and labors alone in his workshop, Dufour produces only about eighteen watches each year. His most famous watch, the Duality, commonly sells for more than $500,000 at auction.

In Dufour's mind, the smallest aspects of the work are the most crucial. There are no minor components, no trivial steps, no microscopic details he won't obsess over, regardless of whether anyone sees them or not. Rivals study Dufour's timepieces under microscopes to find the smallest flaws. So there simply can't be any.

He's spent his life making incredibly complex gears and differentials smaller than a match head and polishing a watch's gold or platinum finish until it gleams. His work is his reputation, so he doesn't cut corners or rush to complete it. Getting that distinctive Dufour finish is *everything*.

Oscar-winning director James Cameron is also an obsessed Rare Breed. He's infamous for driving cast and crew crazy on movie shoots with endless takes and obsession with details, regardless of whether they end up in the film or not. After Neil deGrasse Tyson told him that his night sky in *Titanic* was wrong for the date the ship sank, Cameron asked the astrophysicist to send him the right star field for April 15, 1912, at 4:20 a.m., and the director put a new sky in the DVD release of the movie. "People call me a perfectionist," Cameron is reported to have said, "but I'm not. I'm a rightist. I do something until it's right, and then I move on to the next thing."

› How to Own This Mantra

None of us knows what small detail of our work will be the one that cinches our fame or dooms us to failure. Insignificant things become significant when they succeed or fail. After all, the Apollo 13 explosion nearly killed three astronauts because a few inches of the spacecraft's *fourteen miles* of wiring got damaged.

That's why it matters to take pride in your work. True artisanship feels *special*. It's personal and satisfying to hold something in your hands—a pair of jeans, a letterpress book, a bottle of microbrewed beer—and know that a ton of personal care, attention, and knowledge went into creating it.

Contrast that with being served a lukewarm meal at a restaurant, or having your new shirt fall apart two weeks after you bought it, or being sent a keynote presentation full of errors. A whole lot of people don't really care about what they do, so caring more is an advantage.

Don't underestimate the power of these questions:

- ➔ Do I stand proudly behind my work?
- ➔ Where should I heighten my standards?
- ➔ What does my stamp *mean*?
- ➔ How can I help others be proud of their work?
- ➔ What areas of my work do I need to be more thoughtful about?
- ➔ How can I be better today than I was yesterday?
- ➔ What is my definition of excellence?
- ➔ What is my signature trademark?

Everything that you do, pathetic or awesome, has your name on it. Every job is a self-portrait. Own it. Do it right. Be proud of it. Put your stamp on it. Reputation is hard to rebuild once it's lost.

16

TRY 960 TIMES

At sixty years old, Cha Sa-soon had never learned to drive. This might not have been a problem had she lived in one of South Korea's many large cities, but she didn't. She lived alone in the tiny mountain-ringed village of Sinchon, about 110 miles from Seoul. Tired of the isolation, she finally decided to try for her driver's license; but as you can imagine, making up for all that lost time wasn't easy. The woman known as "Grandma Cha Sa-soon" took the written driver's test—forty multiple-choice questions—and unsurprisingly, she flunked. After all, she was living in a remote rural town and was unfamiliar with arcana like traffic signals and tolls.

What is surprising is that Grandma Cha Sa-soon kept taking the written exam—949 times. Each time, she failed, but she kept coming back and trying again—and earned a passing score on her 950th attempt. Two vehicle tests came next, and she flunked those, too. But finally, after taking 960 tests in all, she earned her driver's license. Grandma Cha Sa-soon's determination made her a national celebrity, and Hyundai-Kia Automotive Group gave her a new Kia Soul. She even appeared in one of the company's television commercials.

In his bestselling 2011 book *Do the Work*, author Steven Pressfield writes, "Be too dumb to quit and too stubborn to back off." Is that the essence of Rare Breed duality or what? When you're grinding and grinding, you never know whether you're digging yourself a hole that you'll never get out of or if you're inches from the greatest opportunity of your lifetime.

The point isn't persistence for its own sake; it's that success could be right around the corner. But if you give up, you'll never know whether one more push would have made all the difference and changed your life. Sure, continuing to push against something that doesn't want to budge is maddening. Sane people don't do it. So it's a good thing that you're a little crazy.

Here's one example of when we tried 960 times, and it paid off.

› Our Personal Maze

Once, a client came to us with an idea for a line of healthy snacks based on—wait for it—the diet of a chipmunk. The idea was just interesting enough to work, but what turned this project into a maze from which we couldn't escape was that the founders were determined to have a chipmunk on their front packaging. Thus began our descent into chipmunk Hell.

We sketched out and explored hundreds of logo and package design ideas based around chipmunks, and every one of them looked like it belonged on squirrel food packaging at a feed store. Crippled with how unsatisfied we were with the work, we iterated until our eyes burned and our fingernails started to chip. We began seeing chipmunks in our dreams. The *Alvin and the Chipmunks* movie sent us into a panic attack.

We became our own worst enemies. We *finally* hit on a visual direction that the client liked, but by then we were convinced that consumers wouldn't buy it. We kept pushing, believing that somewhere out there was the perfect design for this product. We just had to keep working it.

You know that feeling of defeat you have when something just doesn't come together the way you want it to? It was that, but worse. We kept going because . . . well, there were a couple of reasons. We loved the product and the people behind it. We were disappointed that we hadn't gotten this right for them, so pride was in play. Most of all, we felt we were overlooking something. Finally, after months of failed attempts and forced ideas, we landed on it.

Now you can buy that line of healthy snacks, Munk Pack, in Target, Costco, Whole Foods, and many other retailers—with the chipmunk logo front and center. The product is now hugely successful and has a devout social media following. We're very proud of it, which we should be, considering that little fucking rodent nearly killed us.

› How to Own This Mantra

We can't tell you when too much is too much. It might be imposed on you from the outside, such as when a client runs out of time, money, or patience. But when it's not, of course, you need to police yourself. Have things gotten out of hand? Are you falling asleep on your desk? Are you ridiculously over your contracted hours?

On the other hand, what are the signs that you should keep going? Maybe this is the client of a lifetime and you can't screw this up. We've worked on jobs that we didn't get paid well for, but we couldn't *not* do the work. Maybe you love the work so much that you're really not tired. Maybe a project like this one defeated you in the past and it's a matter of professional pride that you're going to make up for it. Maybe the money's just too epic. Then have at it, you obsessive creature.

Part of your superpower as an obsessed person is the ability to never quit. Your goal is to embrace that as a gift, not a tick.

Here are a few things to think about:

- Keep testing, even when it's perfect.
- Even when you win, keep fighting.
- You only fail when you quit.
- Laugh when it's only you and the cleaning staff left in the building.
- Don't get mad at yourself.
- Don't ever phone it in. Every attempt deserves your very best.

We know that some of you work/life balance gurus are cringing. It's true. Relentless can be maddening. So whether you're calling it quits or pulling an all-nighter, take care of yourself. Oh, and eat well and get enough sleep. Your mom told us to say that.

17

DON'T WORK LIKE A CAVEMAN

Naturally obsessed people typically fall into one of two camps: the clean freak or the caveman. If you're the former, you're hyperorganized. Paper clips are lined up and color coded, file names are consistently structured in beautifully organized Dropbox folders, and (like Sunny) you turn your water bottles label-side out. If you're the latter, you're drowning in chaos. Your hair looks like you've been electrocuted. Your pants are wrinkled, maybe even inside out. You frantically jot notes on CVS receipts. You're barricaded beneath a pile of papers, sticky notes, Coke cans, and empty Pirate's Booty bags. You, dear friend, work like a caveman.

All obsessive minds are mosh pits of randomly firing synapses and scattered ideas, so that's why Rare Breeds need orderly, structured physical environments. They keep us sane and on task. A clean, organized space imposes discipline and pulls the mind back from wild flights of fancy so that we can, you know, actually *deliver.*

› A Laser Pointer from the Crow's Nest

Nowhere is running a tight ship and attending to detail more crucial than in the cutthroat world of white tablecloths and fine cuisine. Award-winning French chef and culinary superstar Daniel Boulud understands this. A couple of years ago, we saw Boulud speak at the Charleston Wine + Food festival in South Carolina, and later he invited us to follow him around Daniel, his world-renowned New York City flagship restaurant, during dinner service prep. Both occasions showed us not only why he's built a remarkable global restaurant empire, but why he's become a mentor to many of the world's top chefs (and to us non-chefs).

Great chefs will tell you that the secret ingredient to running a successful kitchen is keeping things clean and orderly and having a system that enables everyone to work as efficiently as a Swiss watch. This is an organizing philosophy practiced in the culinary world called *mise en place*, a French phrase that translates as "put in place." Without order, dishes wind up mistimed or overcooked, people get cut or burned, sanitation goes south, and the customer experience suffers. With order and synchronization, kitchen staff can focus on creating culinary masterworks.

Boulud is maniacal about neatness and order. How maniacal? Well, he has admitted to using a laser pointer from his elevated office, a sort of glass enclosed "crow's nest" perched above the kitchen, to highlight his staff's shortcomings—a dreaded rebuke that sends his cooks into a frenzy.

When we talked with some of his protégés, they told us the same thing. He's famous for warning, "*Don't work like a caveman!*" and preaches this ground rule to his kitchen staff. There are never any exceptions.

As it turns out, order, precision, and organization aren't the opposite of creativity; they enable it.

› How to Own This Mantra

When you work like a caveman and let the little things fall to the wayside, it *all* falls to the wayside. So quit chomping on that granola bar and getting crumbs all over this book; sit up and pay attention. It's time to return to order and *mise en place* yourself.

First, stop equating sloppiness with being creative or edgy. That's a myth. Ignoring the periods and commas doesn't make you a great writer; it makes you the world's worst poet. We've seen obsessed, brilliant writers with desks neat as a pin and product designers with laptops you could eat off of whose work generally reflects the same kind of order and attention to detail as their environments.

Mise en place can be applied to all kinds of daily chores and activities:

- → Clean up as you go, no matter how fast and furious you're working.
- → Wipe down your workstation—especially your laptop screen, because we'll bet it's disgusting.
- → Calendar your meetings, and we don't mean writing "Meeting @ 10:30" on your hand.
- → Prepare your outfits by picking out your clothes the night before to save time getting dressed in the morning.
- → Pack your lunches for the week on Sundays.
- → Create a file-naming convention that is consistent and logical, not random and meaningless.

- Check your work for errors 3x. Then check it another 2x. Spelling mistakes? Alignment issues? Entire sentences left out? Sloppy work not only damages your reputation, but it can also negatively affect your team and its productivity.

When things are orderly, your thoughts will be orderly. Now: *Clean that up tout suite!*

18

BE LOYAL TO THE NIGHTMARE

In Joseph Conrad's *Heart of Darkness*, the protagonist, Charlie Marlow, has finally found the subject of his obsession, the ivory hunter Mr. Kurtz, in the heart of Africa, but Kurtz is corrupt and insane. Nevertheless, Marlow chooses to stay with Kurtz rather than return to the company that sent him, saying, "I did not betray Mr. Kurtz—it was ordered I should never betray him—it was written I should be loyal to the nightmare of my choice."

Humans are creatures of contrast; the obsessive even more so. Without the bloody-knuckled *commitment* it takes to get what we want, the final product just isn't as satisfying. Truth be told, obsessed Rare Breeds actually savor the personal hardship: pulling all-nighters, doing backbreaking labor on a farmstead, traveling three hundred days a year. The suffering is an indispensable part of the experience. It doesn't feel great in the moment, but it's what makes cashing the check or standing back to see the marvel we've created *so* much sweeter.

Part of being a naturally obsessed person is the obligation we feel to power through the brutal times. In "The Value of Suffering," a terrific 2013 op-ed in the *New York Times*, English essayist Pico Iyer wrote about the *privilege* of experiencing pain on the way to a goal: "I once met a Zen-trained painter in Japan, in his 90s, who told me that suffering is a privilege, it moves us toward thinking about essential things and shakes us out of shortsighted complacency; when he was a boy, he said, it was believed you should pay for suffering, it proves such a hidden blessing."

> Smooth Sailing

Sisters Emma Teal Laukitis and Claire Neaton know that good sailors are made in rough waters. They grew up in the Aleutian Islands of Alaska and began working on their family's commercial fishing boat in the Bering Sea when their friends were in elementary school. Their respect for the fisher's life, and the breathtaking but fragile isolated communities around them, led them to create Salmon Sisters, a lifestyle apparel brand inspired by the unique nautical tradition and fishing culture of the North Pacific.

They spend half their year on land grinding in the business, and they spend the other half on the ocean, fishing for salmon and halibut. There, as they write on their web page, they experience "long days of endless sunlight and salt spray—the routine of pulling on raingear and boots, setting the net, picking the net, salmon for breakfast, lunch, and dinner, and a little sleep in between. When the fishing is good, sleep is secondary."

Laukitis and Neaton wouldn't trade the grueling, sometimes life-risking voyages for all the wealth in the world. Risk and reward are ingrained in their family's values; having a good run or striking out is a gamble. The constant struggle—which includes doing what's best for the earth and keeping things local (like paying more so their product can be made in Alaska)—is what makes them who they are. They know, as all Rare Breeds do, that hardship and pain have important things to teach us.

"I know it sounds really odd, but we all sort of, like, revel when it's really shitty," says Neaton. "We just like it when everything is stacked against you, and it couldn't get any worse, and then it will." Even if you're telling yourself *I'd like things to be easier this time, if you don't mind*, it's still a perverse, visceral thrill to find yourself tested to the max, pushed beyond your limits to a place where everything is stripped away except for surviving the moment.

As contradictory as it sounds, the nightmare keeps the obsessed supercharged. Running face-first into the hard, cold cost of what you want shatters your illusions, dissolves your sense of entitlement, and keeps you humble. *This is what you have to do to get what you dream about*, the nightmare says. *And once you choose, there's no turning back.* Not for Marlow. Not for the Salmon Sisters. Not for us. Not for you.

› How to Own This Mantra

It's all one big test, isn't it? The more ambitious your dream, the more you're going to crash into your own personal heart of darkness to achieve it. You will hurt like hell and run into walls. Alligators will be guarding the moat around all objects of your affection. Sinkholes will be threatening to open at any moment under your feet. Thieves will steal your money, ideas, maybe even your soul. Your lover will throw your clothes on the lawn the night before a big presentation. Three of your top people will quit in the same week. Despite your best efforts, things will fall apart in ways that make you spread your arms, throw your head back, and wail.

The good thing is, once you have that hardscrabble mentality in place, you can prepare for when the fish don't bite. As Laukitis said,

"You have to save your money, anticipating that every year won't be a good year." Sure enough, in 2016, Laukitis and Neaton experienced one of their worst salmon seasons. "It was really hard on people," Laukitis said, "especially those trying to make payments on their boat." But they survived.

No matter what life shoves at you, commit to the journey. Keep a stash of Tums and Cabernet. Find good, hopeful, strong people to brave the winds with you, as long as they're game for the black eyes too. Years from now when you look back and reflect on your journey, the rough parts, when you were sleeping on the floor and living on canned soup, will be the times you're most proud of.

VIRTUE 4

HOT-BLOODED

Passionate. Mercurial. Intense. Impulsive. Fiery.

An asset when a deep love for what you do pushes you to accomplish, work with enthusiasm, inspire others, and pursue a path with unrelenting fire.

A weakness when passion turns into mood swings, rage, or harmful sacrifice, causing you to fly off the handle and turn everyone within range into your victim.

Jack Kerouac channeled the hot-blooded spirit in his masterpiece *On the Road* when he wrote, "The only people for me are the mad ones, the ones who are mad to live, mad to talk, mad to be saved, desirous of everything at the same time, the ones who never yawn or say a commonplace thing, but burn, burn, burn like fabulous yellow roman candles exploding like spiders across the stars."

Tempestuous, piercing, unbridled passion. We all crave it. But for most of us, discovering our passion feels like a luxury for which we don't have time. We surrender to the demands of work, life's distractions, and the expectations of others instead of seeking out that thing that sets our soul on fire.

How many people do you know who feel underutilized, unappreciated, underwhelmed, and unmotivated? They might not know what a passionate life feels like, but they sure spend a lot of time wishing they had one. Work leaves them with just enough energy at the end of the week to engage with their phones instead of each other. They dread Mondays and doze through weekends. Inertia handcuffs them to jobs that aren't even interesting enough to hate. Life is an ambivalent shrug, a colorless vale of "Meh."

Before they know it, they're years into a life that looks and feels nothing like the heart-throbbing, grand adventure they once imagined. By the time they figure this out, they have obligations and responsibilities that make it dangerously easy to stay in place. *Next year, I'll do what I've always wanted to. Next year, I'll chase that dream.* But next year never comes.

Hot-blooded Rare Breeds are different. They *lust* for life. They swallow it like wine in huge, gasping gulps and welcome it in all its unruly shapes: drama, heartache, beastly living arrangements, and wild career aspirations that send them hurtling into God-knows-what kind of trouble. It doesn't always matter if the goal is reached . . . or even if there is one. What matters is *how alive they feel*. What matters is that whatever they do, they do it while bellowing their version of Walt Whitman's barbaric *yawp* to the heavens.

Think Romeo and Juliet. Sure, they made one terrible decision after another, but the intensity of their passion and willingness to defy fate remains unmatched in literature. Sure, they were reckless, but they *lived* for something. That's certainly rare in the professional world, and it's a lot more than most of us can say.

You too were born with that white-hot intensity. It runs your life, sometimes in destructive ways. Kerouac would've loved you. Maybe you've tried to bank that flame down to embers because it's so hard to control. Maybe your temper pulls you into unwinnable fights, or your enthusiasm gets ahead of your good sense and you end up battered and bruised. Still, that fire is powerful. But can you do anything positive with a force that's so chaotic and unpredictable?

Yes. In fact, you can do damned near anything. Meet us after dark in the garden, on the balcony, and we'll show you.

> I too am not a bit tamed, I too am untranslatable,
> I sound my barbaric yawp over the roofs of the world.
>
> —Walt Whitman, ***Song of Myself***

› Life at the Boiling Point

Passion speaks to us with urgent thunder, in a voice that leaves us covered in goose bumps, and demands that we listen. If we refuse, it switches to a whisper that haunts us until we *do* something: *See the world, audition for Broadway, throw caution to the wind, you're running out of time.* It's that thing we can't live without, literally. If we miss our moment, our hearts will still beat and lungs will still pump air, but we'll spend the rest of our lives yearning, wondering what might have been.

Hot-blooded passion disrespects limitations. It regards them as anachronisms, obsolete as landlines. It pushes us beyond the end of our biology and our psychology until we become natural forces incapable of stopping until we've transformed everything around us down to the molecular level. Whether we're sprinting through the rain to embrace a lover or hurling ourselves against an injustice that's become our life's work, passion fills us with unholy intensity. Can you really survive another day without putting your heart on the line, no matter the cost?

For Rare Breeds, the answer is always no. Passion is who we are and how we live. It makes us defy exhaustion and the odds and keeps us coming back again until barriers fall. It lights us up, and inspires people who are looking to escape their indifferent reality and follow us to something raging and splendid.

› The Hot-Blooded Rare Breed

We Rare Breeds shape our careers, and ourselves, according to rules that *we* define. And at a time when technology and culture have handed us the freedom to do and be virtually anything we can imagine, our hot-bloodedness is a compass.

Where to go among the many choices? Business? Music? Politics? Technology? Perhaps something so baroque that it defies description? When we're not sure what to do next, our passions define our paths for us. Entrepreneurs, activists, and artists who pay attention to the free-fall excitement in the pits of their stomachs are the ones whose names we all know and whose accomplishments we celebrate. They move heaven and earth because they lead with their intensity, even though that can make them volatile enough to require a warning label.

The greatest heroes of the greatest stories are all hot-blooded, temperamental, irrational, passionate fools. We love them because we recognize in them what we aspire to in ourselves: an absolute refusal to settle for anything less than a life bursting with exotic flavors and pitched at a soaring, operatic *fortissimo*.

We see that force in the genius of Ludwig van Beethoven, whose love for a mysterious woman known only as his "Immortal Beloved" inspired some of the most passionate and moving love letters of all time—and may have inspired some of his greatest compositions. It sparks in the volatile affair of the brilliant Diego Rivera and Frida Kahlo, whose tempestuous twenty-five-year marriage inspired some of the greatest artworks of the twentieth century.

Hot-blooded Rare Breeds burn like the sun in work, creative outlets, and relationships—enough to make others jealous. We don't have jobs or careers. We have *callings*. We surrender to infatuation, dance naked in the desert beneath meteor showers (what?, you've never been to Burning Man?), and seethe with the hunger for vengeance against those who screw with us . . . sometimes all on the same day. Surrendering to that fury feels like falling in love, and we do it without worrying about the price.

Oh, there's a price. You know that. When you put your passion in charge, you become a tempest, a raging and swirling flame until you simply burn yourself out. You become Andrew Neiman in the movie *Whiplash*, hammering the drums until your hands are blistered and bleeding, desperate to be the best for reasons you don't even comprehend.

> Passion. It lies in all of us. Sleeping, waiting, and though unwanted, unbidden, it will stir, open its jaws, and howl.
>
> —Ty King, ***Buffy the Vampire Slayer***

› The Dark Side of Hot-Blooded

The thing to remember about hot-bloodedness is that it's difficult to control. That's why our culture labels it as a negative, or a vice. People with this trait can have distorted perceptions, ignore the advice of committees, and respond with emotions instead of reason. Still, when this Virtue is used for good—for creativity, for social change, for innovation, for personal fulfillment—the results can be beautiful.

Hot-bloodedness breeds an overpowering sense of urgency that enables you to scoff at comfort zones, dare ridiculous risks, and extend yourself beyond all reasonable limits. That can yield big outcomes, but it can also send you over the edge of a cliff. When hot-bloodedness becomes so volatile that it erodes your good sense and reason, it's a problem. Anger channeled into productivity or ardor applied with discipline can move mountains, but if they cross into rage, irrationality, or a negative attitude, you'll burn bridges or wind up with blood on your hands.

Here are two contrasting examples. When Ric Edelman was a young financial journalist, he and his wife wanted to buy a house. However, they didn't have the cash, so they hired a financial adviser to help them make a plan. Unfortunately, the adviser they hired ultimately ripped them off. Furious, Edelman didn't sue the adviser who'd cheated him or go on a *Kill Bill*–style rampage. Instead, he turned his anger into purpose. Determined to transform the industry that had screwed him, he founded Edelman Financial Services, which has become one of the largest independent financial advisory firms in the United States. *That's* how you get revenge.

On the other hand, someone who lets anger or passion loose without control becomes destructive. We see that in the mass shootings that plague our society, many of them committed by young men harboring a passionate anger that contributed to their violent rampages.

Perhaps, if someone had helped them harness their passions and turn them toward justice, things would have turned out differently. Instead, their rage consumed them and left ruined lives in its wake.

You can't sustain a diet of hot-blooded intensity without a side order of humility and common sense. As a Rare Breed, that's the balance you'll have to maintain. Business, art, entrepreneurship—they demand everything you have. What will keep you going day after day, and inspire others to join you, is the feeling that you're doing something meaningful for everyone, not just letting primal emotions out to play.

Given the heartbreaking suicides of Anthony Bourdain and Avicii, we also need to bring up the link between talent and mental illness. From Sylvia Plath to Kurt Cobain to Alexander McQueen, emotional extremes often bring demons with them. Does that mean creative people really are more likely to commit suicide? Nobody really knows; the evidence is inconclusive.

However, in 2017, Christa Taylor of Albany State University performed an exhaustive analysis of multiple studies examining the link between creativity and mood disorders, and she found that creative people really are more likely than the general population to be diagnosed with a mood disorder like depression. At the same time, she also found nothing to suggest that having a mood disorder makes someone more creative.

What does that mean? That it's wise to be cognizant of the risks of hot-blooded energy. If the intensity of your work takes you to a too-dark place, you need to recognize that and seek out ways to pull yourself back from the ledge. That's why it's so important to pay attention to those moments when this Virtue leans toward self-destruction.

Walk through Door Number One and being hot-blooded is a rocket lifting you to heights unattainable by sober, measured, suit-wearing bureaucrats. But walk through Door Number Two and that same nature can blind you with grudges, jealousy, or the fever for revenge, dragging you down and often taking those you love with you.

The trick? The doors are adjacent and unmarked.

> Don't ask what the world needs. Ask what makes you come alive and go do it, because what the world needs is people who have come alive.
>
> —Howard Thurman

› Hot Questions, No Waiting

The unbridled intensity you bring to what you do, combined with persistence, ethics, and vision, will move the needle and give you the career of your dreams. So, while it's tempting to climb out the window and sprint into the night after the object of your affection, before you do, answer these three questions:

1. WHAT PASSIONS CAN YOU EXPLORE AND EXPERIENCE?
Give yourself (and your career) the benefit of chasing down your passions as often as you can. Passion doesn't always come clawing and howling at us. Sometimes we stumble into it. Passionate about makeup? Broadway musicals? Go to New York City for a summer and apprentice with a Broadway makeup artist. Do it for free if you have to. How will you know what revs you up or doesn't? Why spend your life dreaming? Get out there.

2. WHAT ARE YOU SO PASSIONATE ABOUT THAT IT HURTS?

Finding what you're passionate about isn't the only hard part. It's going beyond the thought *I love fossils* into starting as a shovel bum to embark on an expedition where you spend countless weeks digging in the dirt, living in a tent, and not speaking to your friends and family. Why? Because your blood boils to tell the stories of the past. If you're not willing to tango with all the struggles that come with your passion, then you haven't found it.

3. HOW CAN I CHANNEL MY TEMPERAMENTAL NATURE INTO SOMETHING POSITIVE?

Neil Young once crooned, "It's better to burn out than to fade away." Of all the Virtues, hot-bloodedness is a raw force of nature. It has to be channeled to be productive. All that intensity can lead to burnout simply because work doesn't *feel* like work. What enables you to direct your hot nature into a positive action? Do you have an outlet or release valve for when the fire burns too hot? Where can you focus your energies in order to have the most effect without bursting into flames?

Once you've answered these questions, you're ready for the Mantras and how people who went to the ends of the earth in pursuit of their fury brought their hot-blooded passions to life.

19

CHASE DOWN YOUR PASSION LIKE IT'S THE LAST BUS OF THE NIGHT

Terri Guillemets is a self-proclaimed "word harvester," vintage bookworm, library enthusiast, and poetic insomniac who is "obsessed with collecting quotations, devoted to spreading quotatious joy." She started collecting quotations when she was thirteen, and her website, The Quote Garden, is one of the most comprehensive collections of quotations in the world. "Chase down your passion like it's the last bus of the night" is one of her lines, and it's perfect advice for hot-blooded people.

Most people often don't know what to do with the steam coming out of their ears. Hot-blooded Rare Breeds do. They figure out what is worth chasing down, and then they put every last drop of who they are into catching it. That's how they spin their interests into passions and their passions into careers.

Want to leave giant bite marks on the world? Figure out what you can't *not* do, and then do it.

› To Parts Unknown

The late, great Anthony Bourdain personified life at such a fever pitch. His suicide left us heartbroken, mourning the loss of a one-of-a-kind voice.

Our office in Lower Manhattan is next door to the now-closed Brasserie Les Halles, the restaurant where Bourdain got his start. In the days following his death, his fans paid tribute to him with a makeshift memorial on the roll-down grates of the entrance, covering the area with flowers, cigarettes, chopsticks, bottles of wine, cans of beer, love letters, and other personal remembrances in Bourdain's honor. One handwritten note read, "You showed me that a punk kid from Bergen County, NJ can follow his dreams and see the world."

Bourdain inspired millions with the intense, piquant, unapologetic way that he lived. His beloved show *Parts Unknown* was a travelogue on the surface, but it was really about unabashed sensual experiences. He cheerfully devoured the most revolting local dishes, including *balut* (a duck embryo boiled and eaten while still in the shell) and warthog ass (after which, he took numerous antibiotics), all to get to the authentic heart of a place and its people.

Bourdain was addicted to experience, and not the coiffed, carefully packaged experiences found on tourism sites. No, his raison d'être was to drink deep of the world—to savor a chunk of fresh-killed eland from the plains of South Africa and let the blood run down his chin. Profane, irreverent, intolerant of bullshit, and unashamedly enamored with the pleasures of the flesh, his greatest love was people—people of all ethnicities, shapes, languages, and backgrounds—as long as they had a story to tell and were willing to share a piece of the culture they called home.

Everybody loved Bourdain because he was special. He wasn't just a journalist. He wasn't a dilettante dipping his toe into Paris's Marais district or the backwoods of Appalachia so he could tell all his friends on the Upper East Side about eating a cobra heart. He was an explorer, storyteller, and anthropologist who cared about discovery while not giving a fuck about celebrity. Recklessness, risk, and hot-blooded passion were the driving forces behind everything he did. Yes, his life ended tragically and too soon, but he lived every moment of it to the fullest.

› How to Own This Mantra

Part of unlocking your Rare Breed potential is figuring out the something that you can't do without—that cause, project, or lifestyle that you'll go to the end of the earth for. But let's be honest. This is not as simple as getting up one morning and saying, "I'm going to find my passion before *Game of Thrones* comes on." Most of the time, a passionate purpose is something that finds you, not the other way around.

The solution? Get out in the world. Have experiences. Get out of your comfort zone. Eat bizarre food. Then repeat. In his book *Kitchen Confidential* Bourdain wrote, "Your body is not a temple, it's an amusement park. Enjoy the ride." He also said, "If I'm an advocate for anything, it's to move. As far as you can, as much as you can. Across the ocean, or simply across the river. Walk in someone else's shoes or at least eat their food, it's a plus for everybody."

Every so often (monthly is good) explore a new area of life that seems interesting to you: politics, teaching, cuisine, small business, professional poker . . . any one of a million pursuits that fascinate you. Keep your mind and eyes wide open. Soak up knowledge. Listen to stories. Take notes. If you meet new people who offer surprising opportunities, follow those side roads to see where they lead. (Okay, be smart though. We can't have you ending up on the back of some milk carton!)

While you can, drink every drop of experience out of life. Eventually, you'll find something that consumes you—something you can't imagine *not* doing for the next fifty years. When you find that something, ask yourself three vital questions:

- Could I do this for the rest of my life?
- Could I become one of the best in the world at this?
- Could I make a living doing this?

If the answers are yes, then congratulations—you've found something most people will never even look for: your passion. Passion is a powerful career and life catalyst. It should be the driving force around which all of your behaviors and actions align. It can be a source of empowerment, not just employment.

A few more things to consider:

CONNECT THE DOTS. Let's say you have a job in accounting and spend every waking minute when you're not at that job baking. You sketch cupcakes on your hand, dream of winning *Halloween Wars*, and have bake-offs every weekend. Spend time connecting the dots of why you can't wait to leave your day job to get home to bake. You might decide to make baking your new career.

DO WHAT YOU LOVE, BUT FOLLOW THE MONEY. There is such a thing as a starving artist. You've got to find a way to make money doing what you love. For example, you may not be able to sell your paintings, but maybe you can get hired to paint murals for companies and environmental spaces.

SEEK SUCCESS AND MEANING. Success is a result of your passion and hard work. If you put too much weight behind success, you'll lose sight of your passion. Dedicate yourself and your energy to that which you're passionate about and success will come.

DON'T MAKE EXCUSES. Don't be the person who watches someone else living an Anthony Bourdain life and think, *That could've been me.* Regret is a slow-motion tragedy; refuse it. Instead, find that "I can't live without you" thing and make it your vocation.

Do all these things urgently, desperately, like your life depends on it. Because it does.

20

NEVER EAT YOUR SOUL TO FILL YOUR BELLY

Once, a company approached Motto about working with a luxury brand that sold beautiful women's fashions made from exotic furs. We were still small and looked at the potential $150,000 in revenue and knew it could be game-changing for our business.

We didn't know anything about the fur industry at that time, so we started researching it, like we do for all potential projects, and . . . *holy shit.* We're animal lovers, so seeing the filthy conditions and horrific physical and psychological abuse that animals endure so that humans can make fur coats, trim, and other accessories made us sick to our stomachs. In this case, ignorance was bliss. Being confronted with the truth hurt.

Did you know that about one billion rabbits—one *billion*—are killed each year for their pelts? We didn't. We also didn't know that one hundred animals can be needed to make a single fur coat, and that a hundred million other creatures, including mink, foxes, raccoons, coyotes, seals, and even dogs, are tethered and butchered each year for the industry. In 2013, a horrific video from PETA even showed fur being ripped off of living rabbits at Chinese angora wool farms.

No amount of money could have made us want to be a part of that kind of barbaric cruelty. We turned down the lucrative job. Sure, it hurt us financially, but the business wasn't worth selling our souls to fill our bellies.

› Don't Lose Your Moral Compass

No matter how much fire and fury are in your belly, you have to know where your lines are. This isn't just about holding yourself back when a tempting opportunity that violates your moral code comes along. It's about leaning in to that true north as a strategy for making decisions about what's right and wrong for you.

Just ask Colin Kaepernick. He was the first NFL player to protest police violence against African Americans and minorities by refusing to stand during the national anthem, and he's become a politically polarizing figure because of it. His actions inspired other players to "take a knee" during the 2016 and 2017 seasons, causing national and worldwide controversy. Eventually, he got locked out of the NFL because no team would take the risk to employ him, despite his being an A player.

In 2018, his stand arguably paid off. Nike gambled some high stakes by choosing him as the face of a new marketing campaign with the tagline, "Believe in something, even if it means sacrificing everything." Not only did the campaign cause an emotionally charged, all-out war online, but it supercharged Nike's brand awareness by increasing core customers' loyalty, gaining the company about 170,000 Instagram followers. The Instagram post featuring Kaepernick was the second-most "liked" post in Nike's history. A Quinnipiac University Poll and an SSRS Omnibus poll provided to CNN both showed that a majority of younger people approved of Nike's decision, while older adults disapproved of it.

His career in football may be over, but Kaepernick's refusal to eat his soul to fill his belly led to a whole new life that he never could have seen coming.

› How to Own This Mantra

Don't let the passion for what you do get in the way of what you stand for. We love branding, but not so much that we'll work on just *anything*. Kaepernick loves football, but not more than social justice.

When you're faced with your biggest opportunities, always come back to that moral compass. Does it feel wrong? Your values and ethics are guardrails for the people who work with you. Your adherence to them lets them know where you stand. If you have a set of values you can stand by, make them part of your company, brand, or career. If you're not sure what they are, here are some questions you can ask yourself:

- What's important to me?
- What will I always fight against?
- What qualities are nonnegotiable?
- What kinds of behaviors or actions are never tolerable under any circumstances?
- What is my word worth?

Once you know the answers, make those values part of everything you do. Make sure your colleagues, employees, customers, vendors—everyone—know what you believe in. You can never cross those lines, even if it means failure. Be prepared to quit a project or a job over your core values, if it comes to that.

You can get another job, but you can't get another soul.

21

POUR HOT SAUCE

Your phone lights up at 4 a.m., and you roll over, cursing. It's a text from a work buddy: "I've nailed it! Meeting with the VCs at 9; need to crush this. Meet at Starbucks on Sixth in an hour and I'll show you. We've got this." And a bunch of emojis.

You desperately need sleep, but deep down, you're fired up. You live for the last-minute high-wire act of entrepreneurship. And now your brain is starting to boil with ideas, scenarios, and options. You couldn't go back to sleep even if you wanted to.

If you're in the business world, you've probably been subjected to the late-night, weekend text flurry from a wired-up colleague, flabbergasted CEO, or temperamental creative type who just *loves* high drama. Everything is a reason to freak out, make threats, and send emails in the wee hours. Working with such explosive hotheads is like being with someone who keeps lighting matches until he or she finally starts a ten-thousand-acre brushfire.

Many entrepreneurs, independents, and non-businesspeople seem to careen from crisis to crisis in a perpetual state of wigging out. We get it. Life, careers, and work aren't always pretty. They're messy. We spend a lot of our time watching frantic entrepreneurs and leaders mistake angst for energy, thinking it will motivate people. Sometimes it does, sometimes it doesn't. It depends on who's at the other end of the lightning bolt.

At Motto, we call that condition "hot sauce on the brain."

Explosive, high energy can surge you or your team to victory, but it can also create chaos, derail sound strategy, chase away good people, and compromise everyone's ability to do awesome work. However, under the right circumstances and managed in the right way, that frantic, jittery fire can also be exactly what you and your colleagues need to get unstuck and rev your problem-solving minds up to impossible speeds. The trick is knowing how to turn up the heat, and under what circumstances. If you know when and how to pour the hot sauce and make intensity your friend, you can do some incredible things.

› Last Chance

East Mississippi Community College head football coach Buddy Stephens has got that down pat . . . *ish.* You might know him from the first two seasons of the Netflix docuseries *Last Chance U*, set in tiny Scooba, Mississippi. He's got the kind of hair-trigger personality that makes you startle at the slightest noise, wondering what the hell is about to happen next. On the show, Stephens regularly flies off the handle, makes threats, and falls into explosive rages. He hurls clipboards like discuses and stalks around yelling—jaw clenched, blood pressure spiking—until his face looks like a veiny fire hydrant.

Past all that ghost-pepper heat, Stephens is extremely *effective.* He's the players' last chance to get back to Division I college football—the big time—and maybe have a chance at pro careers. At the core of the EMCC football team are players that Stephens has recruited because they washed out of big-time football schools like Clemson, either for academic screw-ups, misdemeanors, or, like former Buffalo Bills quarterback Jim Kelly's nephew Chad, for "conduct detrimental to the team" (i.e., getting in fights and threatening to kill people).

Last Chance U hinges on the human drama and conflict that come with Stephens trying to "tough love" his young players back onto the right path, giving them a shot at, if not a pro career, at least a college education and a decent life. That's where his explosive temper is both a curse and a blessing. He is a polarizing leader and a cautionary tale, which is why, in Season 2, he tries to limit his swearing and quote from the Bible more often. Better for his heart? Sure, but a lot less entertaining. "I have to set myself up for success each day," he says, "by the demeanor I start the day with and then, really, I just have to realize that in a lot of situations I just don't have to blow it all up. You just don't have to do that all the time."

But, when Stephens pours the hot sauce at the right time, in the right amount, it works. And he has the winning record to prove it. With eleven seasons under his belt, Stephens has turned EMCC's football program into a perennial behemoth unrivaled in the National Junior College Athletic Association. Four NJCAA National Championships. Eight crowns awarded by the Mississippi Association of Community & Junior Colleges North Division. Six postseason bowl victories.

Stephens brings to mind another hot-blooded Rare Breed, chef Gordon Ramsay. He became infamous for his aggressive leadership style and screaming at fledgling cooks on the show *Hell's Kitchen*, but if you watch his online master class, you'll discover the softer side of this passionate foodie, who is touchingly in love with the art of creating culinary wonders and sharing what he knows.

It seems that the connection between intense passion and the demand for excellence can make a person intolerant of low performance and fiercely unforgiving. It's a win-at-all-costs mentality that many people don't agree with.

Some of the players going through EMCC are arrogant, disrespectful, unwilling to work for good grades, and have zero motivation. Some, having grown up either with unbelievable privilege or unbelievable abuse, are at the edge of a cliff, and Stephens's over-the-top ire shocks them into paying attention and makes them realize what's at stake. He pushes them to be better.

Likewise, Ramsay's cooks are highly motivated and remarkably loyal. They know that they're working under one of the best chefs of his generation, and at the end of the day, only the best win.

Sure, hot sauce can burn the top of your head off, but it can also make you surge to stardom.

› How to Own This Mantra

We've got no business cooing "Just take it easy" to anyone, because it's not that simple. We all lose our cool from time to time. We've met quite a few people in our careers who pound the table and drop an F-bomb or two (or ten) because they're hot-blooded people who need an ice bath every now and then.

As a *picante* Rare Breed, it's in your nature to get worked up and unleash a brushfire of fury. It can feel like you've issued a wake-up call to everybody around you. When measured, pouring the hot sauce can motivate the people you're trying to lead. But done wrong, it can be triggering, even terrifying. Stephens has led his football team to a lot of wins, but his temper has also cost them games and alienated some of his players. The key when harnessing this Mantra is knowing when you've gone too far.

Our best advice: bring the heat, but temper it.

Think of yourself as a New Orleans chef cooking up a pot of jambalaya. You've stirred in the "holy trinity" of celery, bell pepper, and onions; added your rice, shrimp, and maybe some andouille sausage. Now it's time for the hot sauce. Do you just upend the bottle and dump it all in the pot without thinking about flavor and heat? Hell no. You season with care. You think about the balance you want to achieve: enough spice and heat to make your patrons sweat a little and go "Whew!"

For hot-blooded Rare Breeds, bringing intensity that exhilarates, not exhausts, is about calibration and balance. So here are some rules to follow:

RULE 1: NO PANIC, NO RAGE. If you panic, your people will panic, and that's counterproductive. Remember, the object of getting intense is to get people fired up, let them feel the high stakes, and turn tension into excitement. Panic and rage sabotage that.

RULE 2: BASH UP AN ANGER ROOM. Let your rage out privately so you can maintain an even demeanor publicly. Ever hear of anger rooms? Seriously, that's a thing. The Wrecking Club in New York, the Anger Room in Dallas, the Rage Room franchise (yes, franchise) in Toronto, Budapest, Singapore, and Australia—these are all businesses where, for a fee, you put on protective gear, go into a room with a baseball bat, and beat the living shit out of furniture, electronics, and even mannequins. Someone is making some mad money from this concept.

RULE 3: DON'T MAKE IT YOUR VENDETTA. Even if the crisis is real and it's all-hands on deck, do not make the moment about you, your ego, your need to prove yourself, making up for a past failure, whatever. Make sure everyone knows this is about the work, delivering excellence, rising to the challenge, doing right for the customer, and so on.

RULE 4: REMIND PEOPLE WHY YOU'RE DOING THIS. People need to know the greater purpose behind your turning up the pressure. If you're going to do it, you'd better be clear about why you're asking so much of everyone. They'll be more likely to see the big picture, stop grumbling, roll up their sleeves, and get down to work.

RULE 5: COMMUNICATE. When the pressure is high, people stress. Even if they look calm on the outside, inside they could be crumbling. If you're leading a team, communicate more, not less. We've seen more projects go awry simply because the pressure went up and communication went down. To lead is to reassure, inspire, and help your teammates know they are in good hands. That will help people run cool, and all machines run best when they're cool.

22

MAKE LEMONADE

"When life gives you lemons, make lemonade." Normally, such peppy aphorisms make us roll our eyes, but there's more to this one. "Life gives you lemons" means that sometimes, life kicks you in the teeth so hard you don't think you'll ever get back up. Someone doubts or betrays you so badly that all you can feel is hurt and rage.

But you're far from helpless. Obstacles that seem insurmountable are what keep you soldiering on. You have something called *grit*. It's the tenacity to get to your feet no matter how hard you get knocked down, paired with the belief that you're standing not just because you're stubborn but because you're stronger and more resilient than you think. Grit lets you channel the anger and pain so you can rise like a phoenix and clap back hard at the doubters. If you want to lead in this disorienting storm front of a world, you need grit.

That's especially critical for us hot-blooded Rare Breeds, because our passions often lead us to soaring ideas and grand challenges that come with vertigo-inducing risks. And sometimes, despite all our talent and fire and drive, things fall apart. The funding doesn't come through. The prototype fails. The payment you're waiting on from a client doesn't come through. It's important to acknowledge that yes, it can and will happen to you. At some point, life will dump a truckload of lemons all over your front lawn.

Admitting that doesn't make you defeatist or a pessimist. It makes you wise enough to cop to reality, and strong enough that you don't need to hide behind self-delusion. After all, as George Eliot wrote in *Adam Bede*, "Deep, unspeakable suffering may well be called a baptism, a regeneration, the initiation into a new state." When the competition steals your entire website, you won't be paralyzed by or blinded by rage. You'll be ready to mix up some mighty fine lemonade.

› Moving Beyond Rage

If there's a patron saint of using grit to turn rage into victory, it's Beyoncé. She's one of the most ferociously original talents in pop culture; her take-no-prisoners alter ego Sasha Fierce is hot-blooded passion personified. But nobody really knew the depths of her pain or power until 2016, when she dropped her game-changing "visual album" *Lemonade*.

The title is a callback to the old aphorism, but the record is an ambitious eleven-part song cycle about betrayal, revenge, forgiveness, and redemption. It's full of lyrical vitriol about "Becky with the good hair," vocals from brilliant guest artists like Kendrick Lamar, and epic tracks like "Formation." But look past the visuals and political, racial, and social statements and you find a woman going public with a very private agony: the betrayal and humiliation of Jay-Z's infidelity.

The courage alone to do that is humbling.

But what's amazing about *Lemonade* is that Beyoncé took deep pain and anger and, rather than deny or wallow in them, leveraged both to create a masterpiece—a masterpiece that also made it very clear how she had been betrayed, and by whom. To borrow from Hemingway, she was "hard and clear about what hurts."

She could have chosen differently. After the story broke, she could have let her rage go on a rampage, trashing Jay-Z in the press, filing for divorce, and swearing vengeance. Nobody would have blamed her. But she didn't. She knew that if she had given into her wrath, she would have become a victim, and Beyoncé ain't *nobody's* victim.

Instead, she channeled her fury into something bigger, grander. With *Lemonade*, Beyoncé showed everyone that power doesn't come from denying pain and anger, but from making it clear that they won't hold you back. In doing so, she lifted herself up not only as a figure of courage, but as a role model for all women, by teaching us how to rise.

› How to Own This Mantra

You're a hot-blooded Rare Breed, so intensity is already seething just beneath your skin. With the right provocation, it can burst into rage. But even righteous rage, left unchecked, destroys everything. Making lemonade is about redirecting rage and hurt and using them as inspiration and fuel for coming back stronger and more powerful than before.

However, you can't rise from the ashes until you admit that there *are* ashes. That's where recovery starts. Don't pretend that you're immune to business failure or personal betrayal, because they will happen, and they will devastate you. But the path to recovery and comeback runs through the pain.

Don't waste time being shocked that you, of all people, were in the path of the lemon truck. In a 2016 article in *Harvard Business Review* called "Resilience Is About How You Recharge, Not How You Endure," authors Shawn Achor and Michelle Gielan found that recovery after a negative event depends less on resilience and more on how well people recharge and move ahead. Accept the pain, and you'll give yourself time to heal.

It's also not a bad idea to assemble a recovery kit:

- → Good friends who will listen but not let you wallow
- → The makings of a good cocktail, if that's your thing
- → An ass-kicking publicist
- → A file of positive reviews, client praise, awards, or other things that remind you that you do *not* suck
- → Lots of puppies and kittens

After the sky falls, your comeback will depend on the details: who hurt you and why, the extent of the damage, how public it was, and so on. You won't know those details until you're picking up the pieces, and that's okay. Grit isn't about specifics. It's about spirit.

Get to your knees, and then to your feet. But always make your comeback on your terms. Never give the bastards the satisfaction of seeing you torch everything. That lets them know they got to you, that you're playing the game on their terms. You're a Rare Breed, and that means you *change* the game.

That's what Beyoncé did. By stunning the world with *Lemonade*, she didn't just start a conversation; she changed the conversation. Nobody was saying, "Poor Beyoncé." They were marveling at her strength. Two Grammys, a Peabody Award, millions of copies sold, and a Netflix documentary later, there's no doubt who came out on top. That's grit. That's whipping up a batch of lemonade.

23

SAY YES

Sunny's dad, Danny Bonnell, was in the army. Danny served with a guy who was a professional entertainer and was scheduled to perform with Johnny Cash and Patsy Cline in a USO show. But the guy was a no-show, and the platoon sergeant, desperate to find a replacement, shouted to the guys assembled in the barracks, "Hey, can any of you shitheads sing?"

Freeze-frame that moment.

You're Danny, sitting in the barracks along with dozens of other young guys all trying their best to do their time in the military without getting into too much trouble. That means *not* standing out. All your instincts are screaming at you to shut up and keep quiet. But of course, you're Sunny's father, so you don't listen.

Danny stood up and said, "Uh, yes sir, I can."

The sarge snapped, "Get your ass ready, Private Bonnell—you're up in an hour!" Danny performed later that day with two of the biggest stars in country music. That led to being promoted to emcee of the USO and traveling the world, performing with countless other inspiring stars.

Saying yes, even though he wasn't ready, changed his future.

› A Fearless Woman Walking Around the World

Sarah Marquis's entire life has been one giant, exuberant "Yes!" She enjoyed a wild childhood in the Swiss countryside—climbing trees, watching birds, and burning with an intense curiosity about the natural world. She started slug-hunting in the family garden at the age of seven, earning one franc for every one hundred slugs she kept from devouring the family's vegetables. After she'd saved eight francs, she was able to buy her first copy of *National Geographic*, and the course of her life was pretty much set. She became a solo adventurer and explorer, the woman for whom no expedition, no matter how punishing, is off-limits.

From 2010 to 2013, Marquis walked almost 12,500 miles—from Siberia to the Gobi Desert; then into China, Laos, and Thailand; and then across Australia. In 2014 she was named a National Geographic Adventurer of the Year. In 2015, she embarked on an epic quest to live like the Australian aborigines, spending three months living off the land in the murderous Outback while trekking five hundred miles across the Kimberly. In 2018, she went Down Under again and walked the uninhabited rainforests of Tasmania alone, collecting data about the area's unique species and sending that information to naturalists.

Crazy? Not to Marquis. She says that when she starts dreaming about a wild place, she has to go there. "We do not have limits," she says. "We just limit ourselves." She considers herself to have been an explorer since birth, so denying her calling to explore the wilderness never even occurs to her. She just goes, and over and over again, she finds wonders.

"Go for a small walk every day, get connected, and just do it," she says. "Whatever happens, take a backpack and GO—sleep on the ground in a forest for one day, two days, just try it. Stop talking about it, it's action time."

› How to Own This Mantra

You could have a lot of chances to say yes to the life and career of your dreams. Then again, maybe you'll get only one shot at the brass ring. If you say no, the chance will never come again. The big question is, how will you know?

You won't. None of us knows whether a particular moment or opportunity will be the one that sends our future careening off on an unimaginable new course. So, we have two options: we can play it safe and choose only the opportunities that we're comfortable with; or we can say yes to everything—accepting the risks, rolling with the punches, and knowing that no matter what, we'll come home with incredible new experiences and the knowledge that we can do it all again.

Three guesses which option we're all about.

Most people's natural response to the unfamiliar is to say *No thank you.* But you're likely at a place in your life where you can consume experiences in big gulps until you find a purpose, a calling that gets under your skin and lights the fire in your eyes. If you're not, life still presents you with opportunities to say yes. Since it's impossible to know whether your destiny lies around the next corner or on the other side of the world, why would you do anything else? Why would you do anything *but* say yes?

We Rare Breeds excel at creating our own opportunities because we're passionate and confident enough to say yes to almost anything. That leads us to our first piece of advice: *When an opportunity comes, trust your passion, not your fear.* If it sounds fascinating and crazy and uncomfortable, say yes. Sail around the ocean. Live on a remote island. Work from a tree house for a few months. Do what Shonda Rhimes, creator, writer, and producer behind shows like *Grey's Anatomy* and *Scandal,* did and say yes to everything for a year. In her inspiring TedTalk, she called it the "Year of Yes." What would you do with a year of saying yes?

In fact, if an opportunity makes you uncomfortable, that's a great sign. We learn and grow the most when we're adapting on the fly. Do you think Danny Bonnell was comfortable about getting on stage with Johnny Cash and Patsy Cline? Hell no. But he did it anyway. If you're still not sure, here are some things to write about:

- ➔ Is this something I've always thought about doing?
- ➔ Could I learn on the fly if I have to?
- ➔ Will it expose me to people or circumstances that could open more doors for me?
- ➔ Do the potential upsides outweigh the downsides?
- ➔ Does the idea of saying yes excite me more than it scares me?

If your answers are positive, that's a good sign. It doesn't matter whether you're experienced or prepared, or whether it's a perfect fit. First, remember that you're more capable than you realize. Second, everybody else is just figuring things out as they go, too. Third, courage wins a lot of admirers.

None of this means you should be stupid. Sarah Marquis might be fearless about saying yes to the most potentially dangerous expeditions, but she doesn't ignore potential risks. She's a woman who treks alone in some of the world's most remote places; she knows how to avoid trouble spots. She's even disguised herself as a man once or twice.

One more thing: don't expect to feel ready when an opportunity arrives. You won't be. The opportunity to save the day for your company, accept a new job opportunity, try something you've always wanted to do, or meet your idol never comes along when you're ready. The moments that can change everything come when you're unprepared. You've got this. Say yes. You might not pass this way again.

VIRTUE 5

WEIRD

Quirky. Eccentric. Absurdist. Provocative. Different.

An asset when your individuality and unique points of difference breed wild creativity and ideas that surprise and inspire.

A weakness when the hunger for shock value or bizarre for bizarre's sake alienates audiences or makes products and messages unintelligible or offensive.

Say you live in a place like LA, New York City, San Francisco, or New Orleans, where weird is god. Everyone seems to live on the fringe. Oddballs are part of metropolitan life, and no one does double takes. Green hair? *Don't care.* Men in heels? *So what.* (Love ya Jonathan Van Ness!)

It's one thing to be weird in melting pots that embrace diversity. Practically everywhere else, though, weirdoes are outcasts. Of course, being authentic in a society that cherishes conformity is about more than just flying our freak flag without caring who's watching. It's about revealing and owning ourselves, and that takes confidence and guts.

That's what a study published in 2013 in the *Journal of Consumer Research* called "the Red Sneakers Effect" (please let the person who named this study name *all* studies) suggests. The researchers found that nonconformists, like people who wear red sneakers or pineapple emoji socks to a board meeting, are perceived as being more competent and having higher status than people who conform to the dress code. The gist is that people who intentionally flout convention and stand out—the weird ones—have to be confident and brilliant to get away with it.

That's a description of David Bowie, who, whether as Ziggy Stardust or the Thin White Duke, was like a gorgeous alien gifting us with ethereal music. It's Facebook CEO Mark Zuckerberg, who made a 2011 New Year's resolution to eat only the meat of animals that he killed personally. It's singer Claire Boucher, who is the post-pop, post-genre, post-polish, post-give-a-fuck electropop queen who created her alter ego Grimes because she thought her world-weary, gender-bending, hallucinogenic true self would be too much for the normies. It's renowned, eccentric inventor Yoshiro Nakamatsu, who claims that his best ideas come to him when he's diving underwater and within a half-second of passing out and drowning.

A weird spirit is like wild hair. Hide it under a hat or tie it down, but eventually it's going to get loose and do its thing. When your strangeness tilts toward the wicked and your ideas follow hairpin paths that defy common sense, you can try to go mainstream all you want, but your weird side will eventually show you who's boss.

But if being a daring, creative original is such a powerful totem of talent and ability, why is it so hard to stand up and be who you are? We think we know.

› Fear of Standing Out

If you've been in front of a live audience, you may have felt your heart pound, your knees tremble, your voice quiver. You may have felt on the edge of panic. It so happens that appearing before an audience surpasses even death as a fear many people share. Why?

Because standing out *is* a kind of death. For millennia, humans found safety in groups—in the tribe. Away from the tribe and the fire, walking wide-eyed and alone on the vast dark veldt, humans were easy pickings for anything with teeth and claws. Standing apart meant vulnerability and danger.

And it still does. When you get up to a podium to give a speech or walk into a packed conference room to present your ideas, you're separating yourself from the others. Your reptilian brain screams, "You're placing yourself in mortal peril! Run, run!" It takes everything you have to push down your fight-or-flight reflex and get the words out.

That's what it's like to cop to your own weirdness. Even while your real self wriggles under your skin like a werewolf just before moonrise, it's hard to quell the fear. Standing out from the crowd can be *terrifying.* You're naked, exposed, and holy shit are you ever judged. You're tempted to keep quiet, conform, stay part of the crowd, and be safe.

Uh, define "safe"? Hiding your real self? You might not feel pain, but you don't feel joy, lust, or wonder either.

› The Box

The thing is, in our natural state, we're built of quirks, odd angles, and goofy fascinations. Children are demented sprites with inner lives that are gibberish to anyone else. They sprint from room to room wearing colanders as space helmets. They spend hours drawing mustaches on Barbie dolls (if you're six-year-old Sunny) or hunched over dice talking about fourth-level paladins. They interview their toys, make friends with bees, and are 100 percent sure that Harry and Hermione are real. They're out of their minds—and it's awesome.

When we were young, each of us was like a salesperson with an old-fashioned sample kit in a fancy wooden box. When we wanted people to know us, we opened the box and showed them our wares. "See? This is my anime collection, that's my unhealthy preoccupation with making things out of flour and food coloring, and this is when I spent six months insisting that *everyone* call me Sponge Bob."

Then slowly, something happened. Our brains changed. We became conscious of what other people thought, and we desperately ached to fit in. A parent or teacher told us to "grow up" or asked "Why can't you be normal?," and our courage withered a little more. One day, we became painfully embarrassed by the fact that we spoke fluent Klingon. Then a merciless middle schooler with a scrunched-up face and a critical, nasal, soul-crushing voice wrecked us: "*You're weeirrd.*"

It kept up during high school. Someone poked fun at our red hair, height, weight, clothes, sexuality, that scar on our face or the beater Dad drove us to school in. Made us feel like an outsider. Made us feel *ashamed*. Our individuality staggered. Finally, we slid that box under the bed and prayed that no one would find it. It gathered dust.

Sadly, so did we.

> Never pay any attention to what critics say. Remember, a statue has never been set up in honor of a critic.
>
> —Jean Sibelius

› What Good Is Weird?

Fortunately, we needn't stay that way. You don't have to be "normal" or "uniform." In fact, it's much better if you're not. Think about who earns the real admiration in our society—artists, architects, activists, authors, you name it. Is it the ones who sell the most units? No. It's the originals, the ones who are unlike everyone else, or who come up with a completely new way of doing something. We revere innovators and pioneers because they're different.

Dig up that box of weird and put it to work. All of those mustachioed Barbies and the anime collection have metamorphosed like caterpillars, as you have, into new things: boundary-pushing creativity, insanely cool design ideas, surprising solutions to everyday problems.

The roots of the word *weird* hint at the power this Virtue gives us to break free and shape our futures. The Old English *wyrd,* meaning fate or destiny, originally meant having the power to control destiny, and in Middle English the word was used in reference to the Weird

Sisters, the goddesses who control human destiny, or the Fates. Later, the Weird Sisters appeared in Shakespeare's *Macbeth* as three witches. The etymology suggests that weirdness is a kind of personal, creative magic that releases its practitioners from mundane constraints and lets them reshape reality to suit their vision.

It's time to relish being the square peg in the round hole, the practical joker, the one who goes *there*. It might even be time for you to rediscover that curious-eyed sprite you used to be, put on that Groucho nose and glasses, and run down the middle of the street shouting, "This is me, motherfuckers! Take a good look!" Okay, granted, you may get hauled off to an asylum, but metaphorically speaking, you'll get the attention of some people. Most of all, you'll remind yourself that you're still *in* there and have a damn good sense of humor, too.

It can be exhausting and scary to show this side of yourself to the world, given the relentless pressure to be normal. You may wonder whether there's a reason for all this traffic-stoppingly unique *you*. What good is it? Can you turn it into a career you want? Does it *mean* something? You need it to, because if it doesn't, you're terrified that one day you'll surrender, delete your book of haikus about grilled cheese, and join IKEA nation.

Cheer up. Being weird means you have what everyone else only wishes they had: the imagination and creative courage to rise above the ordinary. That attitude, and the willingness to lean in to this Virtue, is exactly what sets weird Rare Breeds apart.

> I don't think people are fans of me because I wrote hit songs. I think they're fans because I'm a lunatic or a weirdo. The hit songs came out of my idiosyncratic personality, not the other way around.
>
> —**Billy Corgan, Smashing Pumpkins**

› The King of Strange

Once upon a time, before *Sweeney Todd* and men with scissors for hands, Tim Burton drew for Disney. That's right, the dark prince of macabre cinematic magic tried to go straight, even animating *The Fox and the Hound.* But he sucked at it; it was going against every instinct he had. So the House of Mouse let him go.

Most people might cloak their quirks in shame and start toeing the party line to get a new job, but Burton is our weird Rare Breed avatar because he saw getting fired as an opportunity to go full weirdo. Getting dumped by Disney freed him to bring to life a baroque fever dream of storytelling replete with creepy visuals, reanimated corpses, and the unsettling music of Danny Elfman.

Burton's bizarre universes are Exhibit A that weirdness isn't just about personal style. It's about the odd-angled, off-kilter world you create. World-building is Burton's forte, and from *Beetlejuice* to *Charlie and the Chocolate Factory*, his universes are aberrant psychedelic wonderlands where danger lurks like a carnival carousel spinning out of control. But within that world, everything makes perfect sense. The logic is consistent. It's only to outsiders that things appear terrifying.

That, right there, is the secret power of weird. It's why artists like Burton, Salvador Dalí, and Andy Warhol are its patron saints. Yes, having the gene makes you an outsider, and that can be lonely. But when you fully lean in to the possibilities and give birth to a work of art or a new business that makes sense only to the voices chattering inside your skull, you invert the social order. Now you're the cool kid and everybody else wants in.

› Weird Is Your Superpower

Some people confuse the trappings of weirdness—the clothes, the piercings, the laugh—with weirdness itself. You might have, too. But that's selling yourself and the Virtue of weird, short. Being weird is about the mind behind the window dressing, a mind that's quick, witty, penetrating, and provocative. While most people's thoughts move in straight lines, yours move in three dimensions and non-Euclidian ellipses or hyperbolas. You're an original thinker, one of the true One Percent.

That's power because the world belongs to the people whose minds jump the walls of cozy predictability. That's how you get the gene-editing technology CRISPR. Kendrick Lamar's album *DAMN.* David Foster Wallace's book *Infinite Jest.* The social movement Occupy Wall Street. Weird brands you as fearless and gives you a singular voice.

What you do with that voice is up to you.

Cindy Gallop is the poster child for inverting the social order. In your next life, think about coming back as Gallop—a strutting siren who became an icon in the advertising world with Bartle Bogle Hegarty (BBH) and in 2006 started her own consulting firm with the motto, "I like to blow shit up. I am the Michael Bay of business." Through her company MakeLoveNotPorn, she's become an advocate for healthy, real-world sex and rehabilitating a generation of dudebros raised on porn. It's provocative in more ways than one, the most important of which is pushing the envelope for gender equality, healthy sexuality, and self-care.

Gallop oozes eccentricity. She lives in an infamous black-on-black apartment in Manhattan, complete with a Gucci machete, a Chanel machine gun, and an impressive collection of . . . wait for it . . . dildos. The Notorious B.I.G. once shot a video there.

None of this is merely for shock value; Gallop's too smart for that. A longtime fighter for equality in the advertising world, she knows that logic won't get it done—leveraging her God-given weirdness to provoke powerful emotions will. "You can quote facts and figures until you are blue in the face," she says in an AdAge interview. "But if any of those facts and figures worked, our industry would look completely different. Rational facts and figures do fuck all for this issue. You have to make it emotional."

That's weirdness as a superpower. With a mind that thinks around corners, you can solve problems other people don't dare tackle. In business, your product ideas or designs aren't bound by what's been done before because you don't worry about blowback. You can turn anything—comic books, video games, Victorian masks—into a paying career because where others just see unconventionalism, you see possibilities. You'll throw anything against the wall in case what it leaves behind looks like a Jackson Pollock.

Weird doesn't just have to be an artistic aesthetic (not everyone has an all-black apartment). It can also be a strategy. Look at Penelope Gazin and Kate Dwyer, founders of Witchsy, a sort of Etsy for the kind of darkly hilarious handicrafts that might send your eye-rolling aunts into outer space. After launching, Gazin and Dwyer found themselves facing a problem: male designers, suppliers, and vendors responded to them condescendingly, if at all.

Conventional thinkers might've ranted about the patriarchy and then accepted the situation. But Gazin and Dwyer are not conventional, and they hit on a superb, deranged idea: *fabricate a male co-founder.* Before long, partner Keith Mann was born. It became his name on the emails to suppliers, his signature on letters. The men on the other end responded immediately, even deferentially. Problem solved.

Here's your task for making your bizarre side your greatest strength: Don't hide from it. Don't apologize for it. Listen to it. Step out with your dress, your hair, your voice, your manner. Be a provocateur. See how your strange self laughs at limits. See how letting the freak flag fly makes you more creative, confident, and willing to try new things.

Whatever you do, be *you.*

> You have to be odd, to be number one.
>
> —**Dr. Seuss**

› The Dark Side of Weird

We love weirdness. But it can also get in the way of what you're trying to accomplish. We've already said that weirdness isn't just about the packaging—the appearance and mannerisms of being an oddball. That's true. But it can be tempting to Goth yourself out, drive a pink 1972 AMC Gremlin, or carry your pet python everywhere you go, draw the line there, and say, "Well, that's it. I'm weird." Uh-uh. Weird isn't the clothes you wear or other external trappings; it's the content of your character.

Weirdness can lead you down a dark path if you use it purely to shock, offend, and scorn people who don't "get it." Remember, keep your feet on the ground and away from self-delusion. Your weird world is not reality. You can see a version of reality as you'd like it to be, but don't forget that you have to navigate the normcore world, like it or not.

Weirdness is not an end in itself.

> Being called weird is like being called Limited Edition, meaning you're something people don't see that often.
>
> —**Andy Biersack**

› The White Crow

Philosopher and psychologist William James once said, "If you wish to upset the law that all crows are black, you mustn't seek to show that no crows are; it is enough if you prove one single crow to be white." You're the white crow in a sea of black ones. You're proof that other ways are possible. You're a grace note, a splash of color in a bland world.

Your work or your brand remind people about that version of themselves still locked in that box under the bed. You delight people with subversive pleasures they know they're not supposed to be laughing at. Audacious whimsy or startling taunt, it doesn't matter—it all brings smiles to the faces of people who've sold their souls to conformity. Weirdness makes people outlaws by proxy, and they'll adore you for it.

When you turn your true self loose on the business world, whether it's as a freelancer or the founder of a startup, you'll set the conversation and shatter taboos. If you're still at a place where you're trying on different career hats, being an original character makes you memorable while weeding out employers who don't get you and never will. And if you've made creative work your life, your prose, drawings, or musical compositions will reflect colors that only you can hear, scents that only you can see.

But the most important reason to pull that freak flag out of the closet is that it feels great. You're giddy, dazzling. You're happier than everyone around you because you're being the true you, the one who's not the same as everyone else.

Finding your version of weird that sets you on a path to your unique potential is what these Mantras are about. The people we feature have fed the wonderful strangeness in their hearts and changed their worlds for the better. But before you read their stories, we've got three questions for you to ask yourself:

1. DOES MY WEIRDNESS HAVE STRATEGIC VALUE?

Is that aspect of you also a critical part of producing something central to your career? For example, does your bizarre sense of humor also come out in your design sensibility? If it does, that's awesome. Let those impulses take over, because they'll make your work original and valuable.

2. DOES MY WEIRDNESS HAVE INTRINSIC VALUE?

Even if it doesn't affect your work, can leaning in to your peculiarities help you in other ways? Can you stand apart from the colorless hordes? Can you shine in meetings and interviews and inspire people to give you what you want? Can you simply be a weird and happy person who lights up a room? None of those is a small benefit.

3. WHAT'S THE BEST WAY TO EXPRESS MY WEIRD SIDE?

As you'll see through the stories below, comedic, eff-with-everyone can be used through your brand or your business. But that's not everybody's thing. Your oddball tendencies might be better brought out through your attire or sense of humor, or even kept private, affecting you in ways only you can see. Time to figure that out.

Maybe you're a painter or writer. Maybe you need to see how people react to you to know what you are. Maybe there's just something screaming inside you to get out. It doesn't matter. Being weird isn't safe. Open the box.

24

MAKE YOUR BOOTS KINKY

We know you love your work, but do you love it enough to shave your legs and learn to walk in six-inch stiletto heels? (Apologies if you already do those things.)

That's what Steve Pateman did to save his family's shoe company. The subject of a 1999 BBC documentary, the business in Northamptonshire, England, had been in the family for four generations. As so often happens, cheap imports caused sales to plummet, and it looked like Pateman might have to close the factory.

Desperate to save his family's company, Pateman had to accept the reality that traditional men's shoes had become a commodity that anyone could manufacture. For most of his customers, low price had become the most important factor in buying shoes, because one dull men's dress shoe was just like another, right? Pateman knew that to resurrect the business, he had to dramatically reinvent it by offering something extraordinary, something that wasn't a commodity, something one of a kind. Something *super* Rare Breed.

And that brings us back to men teetering on sky-high heels.

Salvation for the company came in the form of an unexpected phone call from a woman who made specialist fashions for transgender people, asking whether Pateman could make women's shoes in men's sizes. Sensing there could be a lucrative niche market, he took a controversial gamble and began making footwear for transgender people, cross-dressers, and drag performers. He created designs that would comfortably support a two-hundred-pound man while still making his calves look *fabulous*, and desperately tried to get enough orders by Christmas 1999 to keep the company open.

Well, to everyone's surprise, it turned out that there was a huge untapped market. The boots were a hit and flew off the production line, and Pateman decided to turn most of the factory over to producing this new product line, which he called—pause for effect—Divine Footwear.

If this story sounds familiar, that's because it's the inspiration behind the 2005 film *Kinky Boots* and the 2012 Tony Award–winning Broadway musical of the same name, which has been seen by more than six million people worldwide. In the version of the story written for stage by Harvey Fierstein and Cindy Lauper, Charlie Price takes over a struggling British shoe factory and partners with Lola, a drag queen, to start producing a line of flamboyant "kinky boots." In both the musical and real life, the brilliantly bold move to decommodify the brand and do something weird winds up saving the company.

› Thirteen Billion Buck Chuck

With the global economy, it's nearly impossible for a commodity business to stand out. That's why so many founders are infusing their brands with quirky personality and trying to appeal to narrow segments of the marketplace that crave unique experiences. *Don't be all things to all people,* the thinking goes; *be something special to the people who can appreciate it.* That approach has worked beautifully for grocery chain Trader Joe's, which a November 2018 episode of *Freakonomics Radio* perfectly broke down.

The first thing you need to know about the grocery business is that the profit margins are tiny: as low as 1 percent. The second thing you need to know is that there's no brand loyalty; everybody's selling the same stuff. Except for Trader Joe's. The California-based company's business model is unique: run small stores with just a few aisles selling mostly private-label and all-natural brands for great prices, with a lot of wine (including the infamous $2.99 bottle of wine known as "Two-Buck Chuck") and international goods. The company focuses on quality, pays people well, and runs stores where people have fun and feel at home. Moreover, Trader Joe's embraces weirdness. They have products like the Ugly Christmas Sweater Cookie Kit and Everything but the Bagel Sesame Seasoning, and they call their Italian products Trader Giotto's. You don't see that at your average supermarket.

Trader Joe's has about 475 locations in 42 states and does $13 billion in sales per year. We'll bet you love you some TJ's and shop there yourself. That's been the biggest upside of the company refusing to become a commodity grocer: customer loyalty is off the charts. When the first Trader Joe's opens in a town, people go nuts. The brand's American Customer Satisfaction Index (ACSI) score is 86, higher than any other major grocery chain, including Whole Foods, and its margins are estimated to be several times higher than that paltry 1 percent. Trader Joe's is like no other, and customers feel like it's *their* grocer in part because they feel in on the kitschy jokes.

› How to Own This Mantra

It's tempting to play it safe so you can appeal to everyone. Cast the net wide. You wouldn't want to chase away any potential business, would you?

Sounds logical, but it's a trap. Anyone can compete on features, price, or benefits. There's always someone ready to take your spot. Someone waiting to undercut your pricing, out innovate you, manufacture quicker, and so on. But not just anyone can lean in to their kooky, utterly original flare.

Think about the brands, the products, and the people who truly stand out, who define the culture, who are not only memorable but seemingly rise from total obscurity overnight. Like the incredible *Serial* podcast or the crazy talented pastry chef Nick Makrides and his personal pastry project the Scran Line. They're bizarre and weird and wonderful. They became iconic in the blink of an eye not because they followed established formulas, but because they were intentionally like nothing and no one else that came before them.

No weird Rare Breed should tolerate being seen as a commodity. You've got to take something ordinary and make it extraordinary. Here are some great places to start:

PUT A SICK SPIN ON IT. If what you're offering really *is* a commodity, how can you put a sick spin on it to create uniqueness when there is none? Think about how many bottled water brands there are. Then along came a cool little brand called Boxed Water, one part philanthropic project, one part sustainable water company. These clever folks packaged water in 100 percent recyclable eco-friendly cartons and combined it with a do-good footprint. Now it's more than just water.

BRING THE BEST OF WHO YOU ARE EVERY TIME. In today's market, it's hard to stand out. There's no guarantee you'll win a cultlike following or build the career of your dreams. But what you can do is make yourself unforgettable, irresistible, and irreplaceable, every time, no matter what.

DON'T BE BORING. Most people know the basics of building a safe, vanilla brand. Brainstorm a cool name, create a logo, knock out a vision statement, and run some social media ads, right? That might make competitors lift their eyebrows for a second. But what if vanilla isn't your jam? Your goal should be to break out Uncle Carlo's five-alarm chili recipe and cook up a brand that sends the competition into a sweating, gibbering panic. Safe and predictable have been done. No one ever bored people into doing business with them.

STOP WITH THE ME, ME, ME'S. And start the you, you, you's. To relate to your audience, make what you do about them, not yourself. If you speak to who *they* are, you'll matter more. It's unfortunate, but too many companies forget that serving the customer is why they're in business. Steve Pateman's kinky boots weren't about him; they were about the queens.

25

CUE THE SHOCKED FACE EMOJI

In a sedate Sotheby's auction house in London in September 2018, the art world got its ass shredded. One of the works going under the hammer was by the infamous Banksy, who has been described as a graffiti artist, vandal, political activist, satirist, and filmmaker (among other titles). Since he appeared on the scene in the 1990s, his identity has remained a mystery. The ability to remain anonymous in an era when millions of bored kids with Snapchat accounts and next-level hacking skills can dedicate twenty hours a day to doxing you for the lulz is bananas. It suggests that someone is (a) preternaturally gifted at stirring up drama and (b) has a real taste for it.

Much of Banksy's work, from his version of Stonehenge made out of graffitied portable toilets at England's Glastonbury Festival to the group show of the Dismaland Bemusement Park, has been designed to shock. He shoves people boldly into the uncomfortable twilight zone between vandalism, wink-wink-nudge-nudge social commentary, and boundary-pushing humor.

In other words, Banksy has been incendiary and dangerous, and a total Rare Breed. But after a while, even that act began to wear thin. When you're inflammatory for a living, you eventually lose the ability to one-up yourself. When a framed copy of his 2006 spray-paint-on-canvas work *Balloon Girl* went up for auction, art pundits suggested that allowing his work to sell for big money violated the Banksy code of not selling his public works. Was Banksy over? Was he used up, selling out?

Hardly. You may remember what happened in 2018 as soon as the gavel came down on the sale price of the 1.04-million-pound painting: a secret shredder built into the painting's frame beeped into life and the painting slowly fed through the blades, julienning itself into thin strips. The art world was left stunned, gaping in shock and admiration. One newspaper called the stunt "quite possibly the biggest prank in art history." After the dust settled, the consensus was that the whole notorious affair would make the painting—rather, the shredded strips of the painting—even more valuable. The work has even been given a new name: *Love is in the Bin.*

But think about that jaw-dropping twist and the forethought that had to go into it. The next day, Banksy posted a video on his Instagram account that showed the artist hiding a shredder inside the base of a gilded picture frame. The accompanying note read, "A few years ago I secretly built a shredder into a painting, in case it was ever put up for auction."

Banksy's back, baby.

› The Power of Surprise

There's power in surprise; science says so. Researchers have found that encountering a surprise pulls your attention completely into the moment for one-twenty-fifth of a second and hijacks your brain by triggering hypercuriosity as you try to figure out what the hell is going on.

Then comes a shift in thinking as you're forced to change how you've been looking at something or someone. You reevaluate, reconsider, maybe have a total one-eighty. Shock, surprise, and even a wee bit of danger are great ways to win a customer or fan for life.

For years now, we've lived in an age of plot twists, spoiler Reddits, and YouTubers who know no boundaries, so you would think it would be impossible to truly shock anyone anymore. For the most part, you'd be right. But every now and then, someone really grasps the power of shock value to seize attention, and absolutely slays it.

› Cue Big Gay Ice Cream

"Expected" is the last thing you would ever call Big Gay Ice Cream. Cofounder Doug Quint was a freelance classical bassoon player a few years back, which might be the career choice that most loudly screams "Find a side hustle!" Luckily, Quint listened, and he and his partner, Bryan Petroff, opened their own soft-serve truck, the Big Gay Ice Cream Truck, in New York City's East Village.

Now, there's really nothing weird about two gay dudes running an ice cream truck in the East Village. We know that. The two storefronts the guys opened in the Village didn't get anybody's panties in a bunch, either. What *did* make people wait in a line that spills out onto the sidewalk and gush things like "lit" and "popping" on their social feeds was the unusual toppings and flavor names: Salty Pimp, Dorothy (an ode to their favorite Golden Girl), Lunchbox (gay slang for a man's package), and Blueberry Gobbler (draw your own conclusions from that one), to name a few.

Quint and Petroff weren't being provocative just for the hell of it; they knew that in a crowded marketplace of artisanal ice cream, if people were talking about the outrageous names of their flavors, they could have an edge. And an edge in today's marketplace of yawners and sameness is everything.

The brand is just like Quint and Petroff: clever, creative, and filled with drama. And it works—their most popular flavors were picked up by grocery stores, and the suggestive names went with them. Now BGIC is an institution all over New York City. They've even published a book in 2015, *Big Gay Ice Cream: Saucy Stories & Frozen Treats: Going All the Way with Ice Cream*, with an introduction written by their friend the late, great Anthony Bourdain.

Quint and Petroff knew that the shock value inherent in gay culture could win people over by making them laugh—but also by making them feel a little naughty. These guys (and their flavors) are now the jazz hands of ice cream.

› How to Own This Mantra

Consider what will set the people in your world on their asses. From product names to publicity stunts, the goal is simple: to make a population overloaded with stimulus from an always-on world feel like they're experiencing something fresh, gutsy, and on fleek. Build your brand around your story or what your people care about, even if it's weird—*especially* if it's weird.

DEFY EXPECTATIONS. Figure out what the people in your field, your industry, or your subculture *expect* of your category. Then do the opposite. What could you do that would obliterate people's expectations of you while being original? Nothing should be off-limits here—your logo, naming your company something quasi-tasteless. Two fantastic examples: a same-day succulent delivery brand in Australia called Little Succers, and one of our favorite food delivery startups of 2017, Clustertruck. Bring in a team of lunatics to help you brainstorm.

KEEP PEOPLE GUESSING. Surprise people, especially jaded types who think they've "seen it all." Send those people a message on a potato or hire a company to plant funny signs in their yards. In their 2010 book *Switch: How to Change Things When Change Is Hard*, Chip and Dan Heath provide an example: an employee at an apparel reseller noticed that the company was wasting money buying different gloves at different prices from different vendors. When he suggested a change, nobody listened, so he brought all 424 types of gloves the company had been buying into a conference room and put prices on them. When managers filed in for a meeting, they were stunned. Message received.

GO KAMIKAZE. Incremental progress is fine when you're already a player, but how do you *become* one in the first place? You build a quirky, innovative brand that disrupts your category, leaving everyone stunned and scrambling to react. That's what Nest Labs did. When it launched its line of smart thermostats and turned them into connected nerve centers for the entire house, the company forced giants like Honeywell to completely rethink their business models.

When you show up in a way people don't expect or your product is unusual, you'll raise a few hackles. Be the monstrous dodecahedron-shaped peg in the round hole. Get ready for all eyes on you.

26

MIX CUPCAKES WITH CROSSBONES

At the World Trade Center transportation hub in Lower Manhattan, architect Santiago Calatrava's Oculus looks like a spectacular giant white dove rising from the ashes of Ground Zero. The organic, insane-looking structure is a jaw-dropper. Contrast it to the neighborhood's surrounding buildings and skyscrapers, and your mind is blown. According to Calatrava, the design was inspired by a bird in flight after being released from the hands of a child. People, even those passing by or through every day, are never *not* awestruck by it.

Prohibition Bakery dropped some jaws too. Against all odds, the bakery won a huge following in the crowded marketplace during America's cupcake craze. How? The bakery's chef and bartender duo, Leslie Feinberg and Brooke Siem, combined two things that don't naturally belong together: booze and baked goods. Cupcake flavors like Car Bomb, Pretzels & Beer, and Scotch & Cigar positioned Prohibition Bakery on an entirely different playing field from ordinary bakeries.

This is the power of juxtaposition: intentionally binding two things together to bring about the important, meaningful qualities of each one. When merged, their contrasts communicate *something* to the audience. And that *something* is what makes it stand out.

› The Clown Prince of Cupcakes

Just ask our client and friend Johnny Earle, creator of Johnny Cupcakes, the world's first T-shirt bakery. Johnny Cupcakes isn't a cupcake shop. It's an apparel brand that Johnny started a decade ago when he was a struggling nineteen-year-old musician with a learning disability selling shirts out of the trunk of his rusty 1989 Toyota Camry. Now that silly little side hustle is an exclusive, multimillion-dollar apparel and accessories brand driven by a community of worldwide collectors and cultlike fans. He's even had collaborations with Nickelodeon, Sponge Bob, Hello Kitty, and Warner Bros.

How's he done it? By combining who he is with what he loves (making people happy). Johnny is a square peg, a breath of fresh air, a jester carrying a bag filled with the dorkily, adorably absurd. His whacky idea to create a T-shirt brand that drips with pop culture references wrapped in a bakery theme is genius. It's what draws hundreds of fans to camp outside his fake bakery and pop-up events to get their hands on limited-edition T-shirts. It's why thousands of customers from around the world have his signature cupcake-and-crossbones logo tattooed on their skin. Undiluted weirdness captivates like nothing else.

Every time you step into the Johnny Cupcakes retail shop on Boston's famous Newbury Street (which is set up as a bakery to trick hungry people), you walk into Johnny's wild world of whimsy. T-shirts are displayed inside commercial refrigerators. A display wall of vintage ovens open and close with steam coming out of them. Vanilla-scented car fresheners are hidden in the air vents so the store smells like buttercream frosting. Purchased goods are sent home inside branded pastry boxes. The whole experience is designed to screw with your expectations, get you reacting and talking, and forge indelible memories.

Johnny has mastered one of the essentials of building a great brand: it doesn't matter if they love you or hate you, as long as they're not indifferent. Some people leave his stores with a T-shirt; others leave duped and craving something sweet. But everybody leaves with a story.

Johnny's brand pulses with creativity, fun, and juxtaposition. One St. Patty's Day, he dressed as a leprechaun and played hide and seek with his customers by illegally hiding in the bushes around people's homes, giving away free pot o' gold designed T-shirts to anyone who found him. He has popped up in New York City and led impromptu parades around Union Square. Johnny Earle is proof that you don't have to be staid and stuffy and strangled with a navy tie to be a successful CEO.

› How to Own This Mantra

An interesting phenomenon occurs when two or more things join forces and create something unique. It's time to start mashing things together to see what sticks.

Here's how to shake things up:

MIX THINGS THAT DON'T GO TOGETHER. Rapper and singer-songwriter Post Malone has become one of the hottest voices in pop music, defying genres with a style that *Clash* magazine calls a blend of "country, grunge, hip-hop and R&B." Was there a massive demand for that weird hybrid of styles? No. But—and this is something to live by—*there is always demand for the new and original.*

LOOK TO OTHER CATEGORIES. For example, the iconic design of the first iPod was inspired by a phone built by Danish consumer electronics company Bang & Olufsen. If you're an architect, look to nature. If you're a designer, look to science. Don't be limited by the work done in your hood; inspiration is where you least expect it.

MAKE SOMETHING PEOPLE WOULD LOVE TO SHOW TO OTHERS. Johnny Earle has put his apparel in everything from push-pop packaging to paint cans. Even if it costs more, create something that people will talk about, that's Instagrammable, and that people can get excited about sharing.

DON'T GET PARALYZED. We've seen it happen hundreds of times. After an initial period of great enthusiasm for some pretty radical new ideas, guess what happens? Your best ideas get crushed by committee. The more you allow others to persuade you that an idea is too bold or weird or won't work, back to blah you go.

27

HIT THE FUNNY BONE

You're probably thinking, *Listen, I'm pretty weird. How do I translate that to the mere mortals around me so I can win their business but not scare the hell out of them?* One tried and true strategy: humor.

We love bizarre, dark, inappropriate humor. Who doesn't? From *Saturday Night Live* to *Monty Python's Flying Circus*, millions have hurt themselves laughing at innuendo and silly parody burns. But few things crack us up more than the Twitter feed for "The Last Blockbuster" (@loneblockbuster). It's a collection of daily tweets from a comedy account pretending to be the Lower 48's last remaining Blockbuster Video store.

As of this writing, The Last Blockbuster had more than 371,000 followers, who get to see hilarious tweets like these:

> **"Hey people stealing our candy, joke's on you, most of that stuff expired in 2008."**

> **"We're watching Titanic and the boobs part starts in like 15 minutes if you guys wanna get down here."**

"A lot of people don't know this but we own a large portion of Netflix. Just kidding our electricity just got shut off."

"We can't afford fireworks this year but Chad's gonna light the alley couch on fire around 9:30 tomorrow night if you want to see a couch on fire."

Funny is magic dust if you're trying to win a following. You can be bizarre, but it's better if you're bizarre in an absurd, clever way. Great humor is also a sign of enormous talent, creativity, and intelligence, so when you make someone double over with laughter, you're also letting that person know you're something special.

› Write for Sprite

It certainly worked for Chase Zreet, a Dallas-based advertising copywriter who really wanted to land a job at Wieden+Kennedy, Nike's ad agency, writing for the Sprite account. He figured (correctly) that a thousand other copywriters would go for the same sweet gig. How could Zreet stand out among a huge stack of boring résumés and get the attention of the already disenchanted HR person who was desperate for someone—*anyone*—to stand out? Well, for one thing, he didn't have his résumé printed up on really nice paper.

Nope. He got himself a Sprite-green blazer, a phat gold necklace with a lemon at the end, mounted a hoverboard, and recorded an original three-minute rap video about how much he wanted to "write for Sprite." Before you read another word, go Google "Chase Zreet Sprite video" and watch epic lemon-lime amazingness at work. We'll wait.

Funny as hell, right? But the best part is that he got the gig. Of course he did! But here's why the video worked. Zreet obviously has a world of talent and a strong irreverent streak, so he used both. Then, he threw some mad hip-hop wordplay into a cover letter that W+K executives could not overlook and would never forget.

He made himself stand apart from all the other boring, beige applicants and channeled his gift of weirdness—and his considerable writing talents—into something accessible and fun.

How do you say no to a guy with the guts and creative chops to write lines like, "Every single synapse firing up inside my brain will have you thinkin' that the copy Christ just done came." You don't. You hire that weirdo.

› How to Own This Mantra

The business world is so damn serious. Monotonous job interviews. Fickle clients. Money troubles. Stressful timelines. Pointless meetings. Fires to put out. It makes sense—people want to be taken seriously, so they end up acting serious. Can someone please bring a whoopee cushion to our next meeting?

Most people don't learn funny in business school. Instead, playfulness gets kicked to the curb and seriousness gets the upper hand. Sometimes this sucks all the joy out of what we do and makes work a real buzz kill. So being funny or tongue-in-cheek can be an advantage.

Here are a few ways you can hit the funny bone:

LEARN WHAT MAKES SOMETHING FUNNY. Study the work of great comedians, from older comics like Whoopi Goldberg, Bob Newhart, Chevy Chase, Lily Tomlin, and Steve Martin, to more contemporary funnymen and funnywomen like Amy Poehler, Tina Fey, Kate McKinnon, Ryan Reynolds, Chris Rock, and Dave Chappelle. Learn comedic timing, and what pratfalls are the funniest.

DEVELOP YOUR VOICE AS A HUMORIST. Are you self-deprecating, cynical, and acerbic like the late George Carlin, angry like Lewis

Black, or bemused and strange like Jim Gaffigan or Steven Wright? What way do you look at the world that makes it funny?

Your goal is to find ways to cheer up categories that are too staid and conservative. Know where the line is, but don't be afraid to step over it to get a laugh. You can do this by infusing your personality in your business, career, or brand. Chase Zreet did that fearlessly when he sent W+K his video. He had to know that some execs there might see him as a flake, but it was more important that they see him as bold, creative, and memorable. The gamble paid off. For you that might mean pumping up your messaging, your look, your copy, your office decor, or even your résumé. Make your business cards smell like bubble gum. Fill your website with puns. Design an office with funny surprises around every corner.

SEND IN THE CLOWNS. Wait, what? Bet that got your attention. There's a hilarious donut shop called Hurts Donuts with locations across the Midwest. During Halloween, they send creepy clowns to hand deliver donuts to your friends or colleagues. It's a kooky idea that terrifies the hell out of people but also makes them laugh hysterically.

Whether it's gag gifts on a random Tuesday or a team of breakdancers showing up at the company whose business you're trying to win, breaking the routine of the day to make people laugh is a powerful tool.

28

LAND ON YOU

In the poem "La Jeune Parque," published in 1917, Paul Valéry's "young fate" refers to herself as "Thing of mystery, me" (*"Mystérieuse, moi"*). When you go through life trying out different identities, some of them will fit about as well as hand-me-downs. Other rags might look more encouraging, but they'll make you feel like a fake. But that's a journey we've all got to take, because identity is all we have, and sometimes finding it is painful. The search brings up hard questions. When you strip away all your titles and achievements and degrees, *who* are you? What does it mean to be you? What do you bring to the world? How do you show up?

Sometimes you must go through several experiments before you land on that thing of mystery—*you*. It's like trying on fashion, outfit after outfit, like you're trapped in a disturbing episode of *Queer Eye* where Tan France is about to poke you because you can't make up your mind. But that's what you have to do, because it's only when you figure out who you are that you know what you have to do—and why you're here. And that brings us, inexorably, to the marvelous exotic Rare Breed named Iris Apfel.

› Blow Your Own Damn Mind

Iris Apfel is ninety-seven years old as of this writing, and still moving and shaking. She's done it all. She's done interior design for nine presidents, earning nicknames like the "First Lady of Fabric" and "Our Lady of the Cloth." She's had an exhibit at the Costume Institute of the Metropolitan Museum of Art about her inimitable, unforgettable sense of personal style. She's been the subject of a documentary and in 2018 published a memoir, *Iris Apfel, Accidental Icon: Musings of a Geriatric Starlet.* She developed a cosmetics line for MAC when she was ninety; her Rara Avis line sells out on HSN. She's got about one million followers on Instagram. A Barbie doll was designed based on her, for God's sake. You don't get more iconic than that.

But Apfel's claim to fame is really that she has no one claim to fame. She's everything, all at once, all turned up to full volume. It's like she's always been here, in her giant owlish glasses and acid-trip outfits constructed of couture layered with whimsical period accessories and startling giant jewelry that could have come from the estate of a drag queen, or the Dollar Store. There's nobody like Iris Apfel.

She doesn't think about her age, she says, and why should she? She's too busy flinging her brand of idiosyncratic panache all over the stuffy fashion world like so many Mardi Gras beads. Best of all, she's a fount of fantastic advice: think young, go for it when you find something that excites you, and our favorite quotation, "Once in a while, blow your own damn mind."

But the piece of wisdom that syncs most clearly with this Mantra (and that Apfel shares in her book) is this: *care about your own opinion above anyone else's.* "I never tried to fit in. It's not that I went out of my way to be a rebel or do things that were not socially acceptable . . . but I learned early on that I have to be my own person to be content," she writes. "If you have to be all things to all people, you end up being 'nothin' to nobody."

How to Own This Mantra

We all have that impulse to fit in and win the approval of others. Even Rare Breeds have it. But while that desire might be strong sometimes, you have to keep trying to figure out who you are. And you have to ultimately understand that your opinion has to be the only one that matters.

That's why Iris Apfel finds her iconic personal style so powerful. As she says, "When you don't dress like everyone else, you don't have to think like everyone else."

You don't have to find your identity tomorrow, but start looking today. Ask yourself how each identity makes you feel. Authentic or artificial? What version of you frees you to be you and to not think—or act—like everybody else?

Most important, what do you want your career and life to look like in the future, and what version of yourself is most likely to get you there? Keep in mind that identity might not be one that feels comfortable or safe to you. It might not be the one that everyone else approves of either. But as Apfel says, that doesn't matter. Your own opinion matters most.

29

BREAK TABOOS

We really, really struggled not to call our write-up of Miki Agrawal a "period piece." Why should that be funny? We'll explain.

Agrawal, who cheerfully strides over lines and into forbidden territory without a second thought, found herself infuriated about feminine hygiene products and the taboos associated with them. To be specific, she thought it was stupid that nobody had ever done anything to make undergarments better at dealing with Aunt Flo. The whole repressed scene was ripe for fuckery, so she got busy.

In 2011, Miki, her twin sister Radha, and their friend Antonia Saint Dunbar founded THINX, which makes washable underwear that replace the need for traditional pads and tampons. Women loved the brand's period-proof products and free spirit, so they helped THINX hit $40 million in sales in 2017.

But of course, we're talking about Americans and their taboos, and few things are as off-limits to speak about more than ladyparts. In 2015, THINX ran headlong into classic prudish bullshit: outdoor advertising company Outfront Media refused to run the company's out-of-home subway ads because the models had exposed skin and the artful use of food imagery (piece of grapefruit, egg yolk) made them "too suggestive" and "inappropriate."

Sorry, that sound you heard was our eyes rolling.

Agrawal pushed back, saying that the ads were at least as appropriate as the objectifying ads showing lots of skin that ran in the subways, including ones for plastic surgeons selling breast augmentation. She took her case to social media. After women shared their outrage, the original ads were approved. Imagine that.

› Taboos Represent Opportunity

Agrawal has shown that there's great power in being willing to break taboos, as long as you're also willing to deal with the blowback. "From a creative perspective, it's one of the greatest challenges to break a taboo using creative product innovation, beautiful aesthetics, and the right language," she told us in an interview. "There's nothing more interesting than to figure out what are the buttons that people have around taboos from a creative perspective, a design perspective, a product perspective, a language perspective. How do you push the right levers?"

For Agrawal, that approach certainly paid off when she turned her attention to the bigger conversation: period-shaming—the fact that women are made to feel ashamed of their periods, which is considered "taboo." The word *taboo* even comes from various Polynesian words that mean "forbidden"—but also "sacred" or "consecrated." So even though many cultures consider menstruating women to be forbidden and unclean, a woman's period can also make her sacred. To Agrawal, the whole subject was begging to be dragged into the light.

"The reason I was so interested in this category was that the conversation about periods was just not had," she told us. "My parents never told me about my period; my sister told me about it. It's a very uncomfortable subject for women to talk about. It was crazy to me that . . . the most uncomfortable thing that we can talk about is this thing that creates human life."

As you may have guessed, Agrawal goes after everything that's too "weird" and uncomfortable for people to talk about. "Everybody talking about periods is cool now," she said, "and I feel proud of that work."

Her latest foray into taboo territory involves a quirky bidet brand called Tushy, which she launched at a gala where guests drank Moscow Mules sprayed from a bidet while a male model lay naked on a table so an artist could paint a picture on his buttocks. Yeah, you could describe Agrawal as provocative.

But here's the thing: there's always a bigger mission. "With Tushy, we've helped over twelve thousand families gain access to clean sanitation," she says. "We're really proud to support an organization called Samagra that helps build clean latrines sustainably all over India."

But one of Agrawal's greatest insights is that where there's a taboo, there's probably a business opportunity, because there's an audience desperate for change. "It's baffling to me that taboos exist," she continues. "Why is that a taboo at all? We should be living in a world where people are free to share what they want to share. We live in a world where we can't talk about things? It doesn't make any sense. To talk about things not only elevates humanity, but there's an opportunity from a business perspective."

› How to Own This Mantra

The awesomeness of what Miki Agrawal does comes from being willing to "go there" and address taboos fearlessly, even with relish. You can't be a taboo breaker if you're apologizing for it at the same time.

Know that if you break taboos, you're going to start a dialogue, possibly an intense one. The goal is to get the taboo subject out of the shadows and remove the shame or secrecy behind it to rob it of its power.

If you're entering a taboo space where nobody is talking about something, there's probably not a lot of innovation there, so you can do something interesting. Busting taboos and turning them into businesses is a mindset more than anything else.

Figure out where the greater opportunity lies in breaking the taboo. Will doing so gain you publicity and that's it? If that's what you're after, that's fine. But if there's a chance to brand yourself as a champion of truth, or sell products that solve the problem the taboo is hiding, like Agrawal did, that's even better.

VIRTUE 6

HYPNOTIC

Charismatic. Persuasive. Manipulative. Influential. Seductive.

An asset when your innate charm and charisma are used to blow people's minds, captivate an audience, and empower people to overcome fear or doubt.

A weakness when applied to selfish, Machiavellian manipulation—spreading lies, breaking trust, and turning people into puppets.

If convincing someone to eat broken glass is the ultimate act of persuasion, then renowned British mentalist, hypnotist, and illusionist Derren Brown is the master.

In his 2016 Netflix smash *Miracle*, Brown instructed an audience member to eat a broken lightbulb. "It's safe to swallow as long as you've crunched down all the big bits," he warned. "Don't tell yourself, 'This is dangerous, I'm gonna cut myself, this is awful,'" he continued as he placed the piece of glass on her tongue. "Tell yourself, 'This is *fine*.'" The woman looked terrified. Despite that, she trusted him enough to swallow the glass with a swig of water and a bite of green apple.

Brown then put the leftover glass into a box, signed it, and said, "The next time you're faced with a risk, you can look at this and remember that you took a big risk, you ate a piece of broken glass in front of two thousand people and nothing bad happened to you."

Brown has made a career out of, among other things, the nearly supernatural skill of "cold reading," in which he learns about the lives of complete strangers by observing their habits, mannerisms, verbal tics, and other hidden "tells" before bending them to his will. And while some of this can be chalked up to his formidable skill as a magician, he appears to have an uncanny ability to influence people's minds through the power of suggestion. In *Miracle*, he re-created old-time Pentecostal faith healings as a sort of lampoon, only to have people write him letters claiming he'd healed them. More proof that the mind is an extraordinary but malleable thing.

Maybe you can relate? You're the one who gets the nice table after having a little chat with the host. The one who always manages to persuade your boss to go with your suggestions. The one who closes more clients than your colleagues because you know what to say to make them want to buy from you. You're great at reading the people around you, speaking to exactly what they want, and usually getting them on board with whatever you're proposing.

Did you see Bradley Cooper's mesmerizing, lushly romantic remake of *A Star Is Born*? It isn't just a soaring musical love story. It also gave us the moment when Ally, played by Lady Gaga, truly came into her own as the stunning, heartbreaking singer on the way up. Early in the film, when Ally is on stage at a drag club singing "La Vie en Rose" in a voice that brings to mind 2 a.m. in a smoky bar in Paris, it's not just Jackson Maine, Cooper's character, who can't take his eyes off her. None of us can. She fills the screen with impossible sweetness and magnetism, and in that moment, she becomes a by-god movie star.

That's hypnotic charisma.

Hypnotic Rare Breeds have the power to mesmerize the people around them in a way that transcends mere charm. Olivia Fox Cabane, author of the 2012 book *The Charisma Myth*, identifies those qualities as *presence*, *power*, and *warmth*. Blending natural gifts with practiced skills in speaking and gestures that pull people closer and invite affinity, Rare Breed charmers are without peer at casting a spell or persuading people to suspend their skepticism and believe that anything is possible. If you can tell a story that has people hanging on your every word, or inspire people to do things they didn't think they could do, you have the gift. You're magic.

> A lot of progress in the world is driven by the delusional optimism of some people.
>
> —Daniel Kahneman, Nobel Prize–winning economist

The Reality Distortion Field

There's a name for this power: *reality distortion field* (RDF), a term first used in 1981 by current Apple vice president of software technology Bud Tribble to describe the effect Steve Jobs had on an audience. The term describes the aura charismatic individuals project that allows them to influence people's thoughts, feelings, behaviors, and actions. Leaders wielding an RDF can make their followers see not the reality in front of their eyes, but the reality the leader *wants* them to see—and, most crucially, to accept creating that reality as a personal mission.

Ronald Riggio, professor of leadership and organizational psychology at Claremont McKenna College, has studied charismatic individuals and found that this kind of charm has three main ingredients: *expressiveness* (a talent for conversing and conveying emotions), *control* (the ability to fit your personality to your audience), and *sensitivity* (a gift for listening and intuitively knowing what other people care about).

Each of these qualities is not about the persuader but the persuadee. Reality-reshapers know that success depends on how their personality affects those around them. They know that deep down we all *want* to be swayed. Exalted. Transported into a state where we're heroes who can achieve incredible things.

These qualities also explain the negative reaction that some people have to this Virtue. They jump to a loaded, dangerous idea: *manipulation*. They insist that being hypnotic means taking people's will away or deceiving them for nefarious purposes. And sure, that's a risk.

But hypnotic Rare Breeds avoid this by wielding their power in a way that's not deceptive or coercive, but *collaborative*. It weaves a spell that connects with our heart's desire—to be great, to be brave, to do what others can't—and says, *Trust me, and let's make this happen together.* We surrender willingly.

The hypnotic titans of business, technology, medicine, and architecture don't ask permission. They decide what the future will look like and then recruit fellow dreamers to help them wrestle reality into submission. But it's not easy. Charisma is an inherent trait, but it isn't a gift until you know how to use it.

› An Orator for the Ages

Once upon a time, a little-known Illinois state senator showed us all what it meant to wield that power with supreme skill. But if you talked to the members of the Washington, DC, press pool in the summer of 2004, few thought the young Barack Obama would rise so high.

Senator John Kerry put him in the spotlight by tapping him to give the keynote speech at the Democratic National Convention, but on the campaign trail, Obama didn't care for the political pomp and circumstance. He was unguarded, genuine, relaxed, and truly friendly—something Washington insiders don't see very often. Observers would comment on Obama's superlative warmth and his ability to forge a "we're all in this together" kinship with anyone with just a handshake. He had an effortless charisma that was so familiar yet so uplifting that basking in the glow of his smile made you feel understood and walk a little taller.

Still, everyone underestimated Obama. Until he spoke at the DNC:

> There's not a liberal America and a conservative America; there's the United States of America. . . . We worship an awesome God in the blue states, and we don't like federal agents poking around our libraries in the red states. We coach Little League in the blue

> states, and yes, we've got some gay friends in the red states. . . . We are one people, all of us pledging allegiance to the stars and stripes, all of us defending the United States of America.

When he finished, thousands were in tears. MSNBC's Chris Matthews told his audience, "I have to tell you, [I have] a little chill in my legs right now. That is an amazing moment in history right there. It is surely an amazing moment. A keynoter like I have never heard. . . . I have seen the first black president there."

Obama's words were eloquent and stirring, but it was never really his speeches or his delivery that made our forty-fourth president so captivating. It was who he was when he showed up to speak to us. It never felt like Obama was just passing through. He always seemed to be 100 percent *with us*, all-in, rooted and engaged in the moment, saying, *Look, this isn't about me, this is about you. It's about us, together. You have so much more to offer, and I need all of it. I need you.* He lifted us up.

> We all want to believe in impossible things, I suppose, to persuade ourselves that miracles can happen.
>
> —Paul Auster, *The Book of Illusions*

› Using Your Hypnotic Powers for Good

Ever since you were a kid, you've had that same gift. In school, while other kids sat at the back of the room and tried not to be noticed, you felt compelled to stand up and speak up. Or if you're like Ashleigh, you pushed some random Meatloaf karaoke king offstage while he was mid-song so that *you* could shine with Mariah Carey's "Always Be

My Baby." You savored words and loved the power of a well-delivered speech. You watched charismatic leaders, like Martin Luther King Jr. or Gregory Peck as Atticus Finch in *To Kill a Mockingbird*, to learn how they could get people hanging on their every sentence.

You joined the debate club and crushed tournaments. You canvassed for local political candidates. When the time came to sell candy to raise money for the band, you shattered school records. You ran for student council and won. While other students delivered their oral reports trembling and sweating, you strode to the front of the room and put on a show. As you got older, you discovered that you could charm girls or guys effortlessly. You were the hit of every party, the center of attention.

Today, you're still perceived as a charmer, but also perhaps as a manipulator. That's why this Virtue is often seen as a vice—thanks to all the slimy types who know how to get what they want out of anyone, regardless of right or wrong.

So, who are you really? You're naturally charming, reliably capable of persuading people to do or buy something, and always magically able to make people feel comfortable. Maybe you went into sales because connecting with other people has always been so effortless. Or maybe you're leading a small team as a midlevel manager in a company because you're good at getting people to do what you want them to. But that's as far as you've gone. You're not president. You're not giving rousing speeches for six figures a pop. Despite your charisma, something is holding you back.

Sound familiar?

It doesn't have to be this way. As a hypnotic Rare Breed, you have the power to inspire, raise an army, start a movement, and change the world. You have the mojo to shape reality by inspiring others to see what you see. The world needs that version of you—the person who speaks uncomfortable truths, who can change the emotional weather in a room with a few words, and whose optimism can turn a group of people into a team and a team into a *force*.

That's you. Time to use your powers for good.

> My father used to say, "Don't raise your voice, improve your argument."
>
> —**Archbishop Desmond Tutu,**
> **Second Nelson Mandela Annual Lecture Address, 2004**

› The Difference Between Charm and Magic

The word *charisma* comes from the Greek word that means a favor or gift of grace. The gods possessed the charm and presence to inspire others to enthusiasm and devotion, and they blessed certain mortals with that power. Bringing things up to the modern age, an article in the *Harvard Business Review* by Margarita Mayo notes that contemporary research "reveals that charismatic people are more likely to become endorsed as leaders because of their high energy, unconventional behavior, and heroic deeds."

So yes, being the leader in a company or movement often does mean having that x-factor that turns heads and hushes voices when you walk into a room. You have it. You're the ambitious account executive who could be the difference maker for a startup. A publicist with the skills to talk a *New York Times* reporter into giving your client a thousand words above the fold. An inventor with a pitch that can turn

Kickstarter into an ATM. A startup CEO who can get people to walk through the fire with you.

But there's a big difference between being someone who can charm people with the gift of gab and being a hypnotic Rare Breed who can leverage dangerously potent charisma to open doors no one else can. Hypnotic Rare Breeds *instill confidence in others.* You're not just relying on raw charm to win people over, because raw charm is like frosting with no cake. Rare Breeds marry hypnotic powers with ability and preparation. Do you think Derren Brown does what he does just by showing up? No. He's put in years developing his technique. When he brings his persuasive powers to bear, there's practiced skill behind them.

That's the secret. When you pair your inborn charm with skill, polish, and the intent to help, you flood people with the confidence that they can do what you ask of them—because you have the same unshakable confidence in yourself. They know they can trust you, you have their best interests at heart, and everything will be all right. You're no longer manipulating them for your own glory; you're sharing the best of yourself to lift everyone up. That's real magic.

> Successful leadership takes more than charisma because charisma without character is postponed calamity.
>
> **—Peter Ajisafe, *Decide Forward: The Pathway to All-Round Success***

› The Murky Waters of Manipulation

According to the Brothers Grimm, in 1284 the leaders of Hamelin hired a piper to lure away the rats that plagued the village. The colorful piper did as he was asked, but the leaders refused to pay him, so a year later he came back and lured away all the town's children to an unknown doom.

The moral: collection agencies suck. No, wait, the moral is actually that when abused, manipulation and allure can be as hazardous as they are useful.

As we were writing this book, no word got people's dander up as much as that word—*manipulation*. The connotations are just so negative, bringing to mind a con artist, like Frank Abagnale, who was the inspiration for the movie *Catch Me If You Can*, grinning and charming everyone in sight while pretending to be people he wasn't and writing millions of dollars of bad checks. Being hypnotic *is* about manipulating people, but use that word and everyone assumes you're talking about Machiavellian schemes that treat people as pawns. That's most definitely not what being a Rare Breed is about. However, this Virtue is packed with negative implications, so we've got to talk about them.

This Virtue has a slender margin between light and darkness. The power to change people's minds and persuade them to follow you can be a narcotic. Abuse it and you become addicted to it, and addicts do bad things before they hit rock bottom. It's also important to note that excessive, self-absorbed charisma is perceived as arrogance, and that's detrimental to your ability to lead an organization. A study published in 2015 in the *Journal of Management* of 105 small to medium-sized US tech companies found that organizations with humble leaders were more collaborative and made the most of their talent than organizations run by self-aggrandizing types with giant egos. Some of the worst monsters and manipulators in human history were also some of its most compelling orators.

The key here is your intent. Manipulation and misdirection cross into the danger zone when you use them for selfish ends or to deceive people. For instance, Bernie Madoff started as a stockbroker but he wound up running the biggest Ponzi scheme in world history, defrauding thousands of people out of billions of dollars because they believed in him. Most lost everything they had. A great stage magician, on the other hand, manipulates an audience to delight them. An inspiring speaker can move people to change their habits and mindset in a positive way. A good doctor might manipulate a reluctant patient into taking medication that will save his or her life. Your intent is *everything.*

Remember, it's not about *you*. It's about *us*.

> When you put together deep knowledge about a subject that intensely matters to you, charisma happens. You gain courage to share your passion, and when you do that, folks follow.
>
> —**Jerry Porras, Stewart Emery, and Mark Thompson,**
> ***Success Built to Last: Creating a Life That Matters***

› Hypnotic Suggestions

You can't test your hypnotic powers in front of a mirror. You've got to hit the streets and show the world what you've got. Go on interviews. Speak at events. Pitch your business idea. Do an open mic night or poetry slam. Anything to limber up those persuasion muscles.

Strategize. Before your next interview or meeting, know how you'll enter and leave the room. Know what you'll say and when. Have the answers to tough questions in your head before you need them. Rehearse, rehearse, rehearse. Talent is wonderful, but this is one Virtue that you can and should polish. People will let you persuade them only if they believe you're the real thing.

Four quick bits of advice before the Mantras:

1. CAPTIVATE FROM THE FIRST WORD.

People have short attention spans, so you need to hook them fast and give them a reason to stay with you from the top. Hooking the audience early is necessary to keep them captivated. To do that, ask an important question, make a meaningful statement, or open with a gripping story.

2. BREAK THE FORCE FIELD.

We naturally keep other people at a distance, and that can make it hard to connect. There's usually an invisible wall between you and your audience. Closing the gap fast and breaking down barriers will help you resonate with who they are and what they care about. This can be uncomfortable, because you have a force field, too. But once you get in the habit of breaking it, you'll connect in powerful ways.

3. PROJECT CONFIDENCE AND MAGNETISM.

Great orators are confident. They have to be in order to reach a magnetic-like state. If you let nerves show, the audience will see it. Speaking with authority allows the message to flow *through* you. It enables you to deliver important points without anxiety or jitters. Remember, you are the vessel, the conduit through which your message will be heard.

4. TRANSFER AN EXTRAORDINARY GIFT.

Your gift is an idea, and your job is to plant your idea inside the minds of your audience. But it will stick only if your audience feels it will benefit them. That's how ordinary talks become extraordinary. The idea has no power if it stays inside you. As TED says, the best speeches have "ideas worth spreading."

The following Mantras are your spell book to conjuring up your hypnotic Rare Breed. In each of these stories, someone took a pinch of charisma, a dash of allure, and a ton of persuasion to create magical experiences that inspire and captivate.

30

DELIVER A SERMON

If you're a naturally hypnotic person, public speaking probably isn't as terrifying for you as it is for most people. Matter of fact, you're probably pretty good at it. But the challenge is how to leverage that trait in the most powerful way. Whether you're leading one person or ten thousand, the challenge isn't just to get them fired up but to keep them motivated and inspired. Some managers and entrepreneurs try to do that by giving regular speeches, but that never works. Their hearts are in the right place, but they're using the wrong tool.

Instead of simply giving a speech, deliver a sermon. Before you protest that sermons are only for ministers, hear us out. We're not suggesting that you preach to people, but that you borrow the qualities that great sermons use to get people dancing in the aisles, throwing their arms in the air, and shouting "Amen!" It turns out there is a world of difference between a speech and a sermon.

When you give a speech, you're just imparting information. When you hear a gifted preacher deliver a sermon, something else is happening. A sermon doesn't just inform; it helps the people who hear it see the world a little differently after it's over. A speech might persuade, but a great sermon actually changes the hearts and minds of the people who hear it.

› Stunning the Brits with the Power of Love

One of the greatest examples of this was the speech that Bishop Michael Curry, the first African American presiding bishop of The Episcopal Church, gave at the wedding of Prince Harry and Meghan Markle in May 2018. It remains the most moving, spine-tingling sermon we've heard recently.

What made it so extraordinary was that it overflowed with all four bits of advice we described above: it captivated, it broke the force field, it projected confidence and magnetism, and it transferred a gift. In that way, it was nothing like the traditionally bloodless, dry yawnfests that Church of England archbishops had been dropping on listeners during royal weddings all the way back to Charles and Diana. Royals and guests who were expecting to hear more of the same passionless recitation about faith and fidelity got set on their backsides by Bishop Curry's brand of old-time religion.

He proclaimed. He thundered. He very nearly broke into glorious song as he spoke of the tactile, titanic, unstoppable power of love as a transformative force and a tool for social justice. The Royal Family has a long and deliberate history of being theologically neutral—and more than that, emotionally detached even from events as momentous as matrimony. But it was impossible to remain detached with Curry's rich tenor echoing throughout St. George's Chapel.

Curry hit all the right notes at the perfect pitch with words like, "When love is the way, we will let justice roll down like a mighty stream and righteousness like an ever-flowing brook. When love is the way, poverty will become history. When love is the way, the earth will be a sanctuary." His emotion was manifest in every line of his body and in the sweat on his brow. He told the theologically centered story of a world where love conquers all, and he demanded that his listeners act to bring that world into existence. It was Billy Sunday meets Frederick Douglass, and it was marvelous. Even the stiff-upper-lip crowd was visibly moved; we could swear that the queen herself was *this close* to shouting "Amen!"

› How to Own This Mantra

You don't need to be Michael Curry or a fire-breathing minister to turn "meh" speeches into Shakespearean "we few, we happy few" sermons. First, *stop giving speeches.* Research actually shows that the typical charismatic leader is bad for his or her organization, because leaders with charm and a way with words usually spend too much time trying to inspire their people and not enough time leading by example.

Instead, avoid the Achilles' heel of this Virtue and embrace your inner hypnotic Rare Breed by using the gift of gab to create a powerful sermonlike message instead of a fluffy feel-good speech. Figure out how you can use words to help your people discover their best selves and act in accordance with the values they care about. That's what a sermon does—it makes us want to be better, and shows us how to get there. Ask yourself these questions:

- → Will the people listening to me see things differently once I finish speaking?
- → What message can I bring them that will help them question reality and find qualities in themselves that they might not have known existed?
- → What message will inspire and leave my listeners changed?

→ Is there a personal story I can share, a life lesson I've learned, that my audience will identify with?

Once you know the answers to these questions, invest some time in watching or reading the great sermons and speeches by the greatest orators, from Abraham Lincoln to Michelle Obama. See how poetic their speeches are. See how they use captivating phrasing ("When they go low, we go high") to drive home their points and get their audiences cheering. Take what you can from their rhythm, tempo, word choices, and even how long their sermons are. Then write your own and practice it until you can do it backwards and forwards.

You will want to test your sermon, of course, but we are not suggesting that you throw yourself to the wolves. Try your message on a small group of discerning and friendly people who will nonetheless tell you exactly what they think when you're done. Incorporate that feedback into your words, and then you're ready to try your sermon on your real audience.

Three elements can make a sermon the perfect communication tool for a hypnotic Rare Breed:

STORYTELLING. All great sermons have a profound message with a beginning, middle, and end. If you read one of the immortal sermons, such as abolitionist and women's rights activist Sojourner Truth's "Ain't I a Woman?" (and make no mistake, that was a sermon for the ages), you'll notice a powerful arc. Delivered in 1851, this sermon challenged the status quo, the brutality Sojourner Truth experienced as a slave, and the complete lack of logic in gender inequality before dropping the mic with the ending: "If the first woman God ever made was strong enough to turn the world upside down all alone, these women together ought to be able to turn it back, and get it right side up again! And now they is asking to do it, the men better let them."

EMOTION. A person delivering an effective sermon believes wholeheartedly in what he or she is saying, and that comes through in tone, body language, and energy. You can feel and see pain, excitement, or anger in every muscle and hear it in every word. Because "mirror neurons" in our brain mimic the emotions we see in others, we're compelled to respond in kind. Just watch the chilling speech delivered by Yeonmi Park, an escapee from North Korea, at the One Young World summit in 2014. Her emotion is contagious.

IMPACT. Great sermons elicit strong reactions and responses—from something as simple as praise at church or as multifaceted as inspiring your team to ramp up on a vital project. Either way, people are motivated to do something.

Sermons are rarely comfortable or predictable. They should be challenging, unexpected, and leave no one untouched.

31

CAST A SPELL

In the world of high-end cuisine, chefs rule. They write best-selling books, like Julia Child's 1961 classic *Mastering the Art of French Cooking* and Anthony Bourdain's 2000 *Kitchen Confidential.* They star on reality and competition television shows like *Top Chef*, *Chopped*, and *Iron Chef.* They are the subject of narrative films like *Burnt* and of niche documentaries such as Netflix's biographical series *Chef's Table* and PBS's *Mind of a Chef.* They function as television pitchmen and pitchwomen for luxury products and automobiles.

They've left the kitchen in the dust and become cultural icons.

That's why Jim Denevan's company Outstanding in the Field captures hearts and blows minds. Denevan—a former top-flight fashion model and California chef—creates special, one-night-only al fresco dinners in sacred spaces all over the world. There, guest chefs, or he himself, improvise meals based on what's available in a specific locale.

Outstanding in the Field, as said on its website, is a "radical intervention to stale dining conventions." Rather than bringing food to guests in a traditional restaurant, Denevan and his culinary caravan bring people to food. The multicourse, farm-to-table experiences are hosted in stunning wildflower-strewn fields and on windswept beaches, rooftop gardens, cattle ranches, and other bucolic settings across all fifty states and in fifteen countries around the world. Hundreds of guests sit family style at one very long table beneath the sun and stars. The meals taste uniquely of their place and show off the magnificent effort of the people who nurture the food to maturity.

That might sound like just a really lit night on a prairie or mountaintop, but Denevan wants to do more than inspire Instagram photos. His aspiration is, as *GQ* magazine put it, "to free us from the cult of celebrity chefs and the limits of the restaurant experience."

The current age of celebrity chefdom might be unprecedented, but humankind has been dining in restaurants as far back as eleventh-century China. To free diners from that construct is to treat them to an unforgettable, one-of-a-kind experience.

Outstanding in the Field started in 1999 when Denevan became unhappy with the limited, sanitized, isolated dining experience available within the four walls of restaurants. He spent a few summers creating early iterations, and when he had the experience right, he quit his job, bought a vintage bus, and began touring North America to produce the ultimate experience in dining. He's been on the road ever since.

The dinners are largely improvised and taste, says Denevan, like "an eccentric farmer's idea of poetry. Like hard work." During the meal, the growers address the diners, explaining the thought and care that went in to what they're eating. But what really makes Outstanding in the Field work isn't the ingredients, cooking, or locations. It's the hypnotic spell cast upon the guests.

Denevan's experiences are enchanted, short-lived works of art, and that's what makes them so marvelous. When people finish their food in white-linen bistros, they bounce. At an Outstanding in the Field meal, they linger, caught in the grip of something primal and evanescent. Eventually they leave, the chefs pack up, the tables disappear, and all that remains are the dandelions, the barn swallows, and the guests' memories. Their experience—and how it changes them—stays forever.

› How to Own This Mantra

Millions of people adore alternate-world fantasies, from *Alice in Wonderland* to *Lord of the Rings* to *Fantastic Beasts and Where to Find Them.* We love the notion of being swept off our feet (or tumbling down a rabbit hole) and ending up in a place where we can leave the everyday behind. Where the colors are brighter, good and evil are clearly marked, and miracles are possible. Who doesn't wish they could board the Hogwarts Express and steam their way to a place filled with magic and wonder?

Take that seductive, intriguing quality into your work by lifting people away from the mundane and into the wonder of it all, even for a few minutes.

A couple of ways to do that:

TRANSPORT YOUR AUDIENCE. You can transport with your product; with captivating words, images, ideas, and sounds; with a compelling story; or, like Outstanding in the Field, with the physical surroundings you place people in. But remember, the goal is to craft a unique *experience* that puts people into a dream-state.

The storied fragrance brand Le Labo has this down to a science (and art). Step into a store, and you're immediately transported. The stores use scent to sprinkle magic over your brain's olfactory centers. You're mesmerized by the explosive top notes and soulful surroundings. You watch in awe as the perfumer hand-blends a bottle of Santal 33, ensuring that you get the freshest ingredients possible. The experience is intoxicating—a gateway drug into a different land.

CREATE UNFORGETTABLE EXPERIENCES. This is about novelty, about giving people what they rarely experience, have never experienced, or wish they could experience. Big or small, it doesn't matter. Create other worlds, like the *Alice in Wonderland*–themed pop-up in New York City. It's as completely bonkers as you might hope for. Hop aboard a stationary double-decker bus for cocktails with classic characters from the Lewis Carroll book, all combined with British teatime snacks.

If you're a chef, invite patrons to dine in the dark, like they do in Las Vegas's BLACKOUT Dining in the Dark. If you're in retail, design a showroom that makes customers forget where they are, like fashion startup MM.LaFleur did with its Bryant Park location, by creating an oasis in the center of city chaos. If you're a doctor, dance to cheer up your sick patients, like "Dancing Doc" Tony Adkins of Children's Hospital of Orange County does for the kids he takes care of.

See, the thing about casting a spell is that it *can* be big and fancy, but it doesn't *have* to be. Here's your chance to wiggle your nose and bewitch the world.

32

PLAY THE ORCHESTRA

In the film *Steve Jobs*, frustrated Apple cofounder Steve Wozniak asks Jobs, "What do you *do*?" Jobs replies, "I play the orchestra."

In his book 2009 *Maestro: A Surprising Story About Leading by Listening*, Roger Nierenberg, a veteran conductor, says maestros have three gifts: (1) they encourage others to develop their own solutions because they don't micromanage; (2) they help people feel ownership of their whole piece, not just their individual parts; and (3) they lead by listening. When people sense genuine open-mindedness, they offer more of their talent. If not, they get defensive and hold back their best ideas.

Hypnotic Rare Breeds play the orchestra. Their people are the instruments, and by waving around a combination of coercion, challenge to the ego, raw positivity, a circus ringmaster's glib charm, and a bit of stunt performer bravado—waving it like a conductor waves a baton—they make perfect music happen.

Soul-crushing, blistering work on deadline in E flat? Done.

Innovate by defying the laws of physics in A minor? Can do.

Anything's possible when you can take the disparate elements of a company or team and bring them together into a beautiful harmony.

› Great Conductors

Orchestral conductors embody the psychokinetic power of the great, charming manipulators. Power seems to emanate from the tip of the conductor's baton like it's a magical wand that *wills* musicians to produce sounds that make the heavens weep. Yet each great conductor is different. Some swagger with arrogance and combativeness; others are uncompromising geniuses of musicology who know how to wring every last spark of emotion and meaning out of a piece by Dvorak, Bach, or Copland.

That was certainly true of Leonard Bernstein. Many people only know him as the man who composed *West Side Story*, but he was much more, including the music director of the New York Philharmonic for a decade. A story told by conductor Marin Alsop on the website Leonard Bernstein at 100 reveals the special something that Bernstein embodied. She attended a rehearsal of Bernstein conducting Tchaikovsky's Fifth Symphony, and that day, he "walked out onto the podium and announced to the New York Philharmonic that he'd been 'wrong' about [the piece] all along!" Here was a titan of classical music, a field known for massive egos, admitting that he'd been leading his musicians in the wrong direction. But it was brilliant. As Alsop writes, "This willingness and desire to re-examine every piece of music, to bring a fresh approach and new insights to every performance of a work, set Bernstein apart from everyone else." By thus humbling himself, Bernstein had his players in the palm of his hand. They wanted to be great. They wanted to create something unearthly, just as he did.

What great conductors have in common is that each brings to the podium a respect for the musicians they are leading. They know that to make music happen, everyone must play their part. They might be the conductor, but they aren't the only star of the show.

A Different Lena: Lena Waithe

"Star" is a word lots of people use to describe Lena Waithe, along with "genius," "disruptive," and "gifted." No matter what she does, all eyes are on her. She's got charm. And she's everywhere.

Let's see, she's (deep breath) the character Denise on *Master of None*; executive producer of Showtime's *The Chi*, which she also created; writer-producer of TBS's pilot *Twenties*; producer of the comic dance film *Step Sisters*; co-chair of the Committee of Black Writers at the Writers Guild of America; and a mentor to screenwriters via the Black List, among other pursuits. Next time you're tempted to complain that you're busy . . . don't.

Waithe is one of the great maestros. As a hypnotic Rare Breed, she's done so much to elevate underrepresented artists in Hollywood—not just women, not just LGBTQ performers, not just African Americans, but everyone. In creating and producing shows, and advocating for black writers, she's radiating opportunity in all directions like a star radiates light. Nobody would fault her for focusing only on the progress of her own career, but instead, she's orchestrating gay, black professionals and helping them find their power and their voices in entertainment.

That's what conductors do. They channel their energy to bring out the best in those around them.

How to Own This Mantra

Jack Welch wrote in his 2005 book *Winning*, "When you become a leader, success is all about growing others." The critical skill of any conductor is to create harmony among the group, but it's also about nurturing others. When you're standing before your orchestra (your team, partners, colleagues), you might have one hundred individual instruments, played by phenomenally skilled players who all need to come together to realize a vision. Make the wrong move and you have cacophony. Make the right choices, invite everyone to blend in to one harmonic texture, and you have music.

How do you get all your people playing the same piece of music in harmony? How do you get them to complement, not sabotage each other? How do you make a group of people more than the sum of its parts?

To take full advantage of your talents, you'll want to emulate the qualities that orchestral conductors bring to the table in order to lead a symphony orchestra. We call them *mastery*, *authority*, *attention*, and *generosity*.

MASTERY. A conductor must be a master musician. Before you can lead and inspire others, you need to know as much as you can about every facet of the field you're in. Lena Waithe has been an actor, writer, producer, executive producer, and labor leader to date, and there's little doubt that she'll add director to her résumé in the near future. Aspire to be that well-rounded as an entrepreneur, independent, activist, artist, or executive. That will give you both knowledge and the next quality, authority.

AUTHORITY. Conductors exert absolute control over the ensemble. The people you lead will expect you to tell them where to go and what to do. You don't have to think for them, but you will need to set their expectations. If you're mentoring fellow independents, have career or income goals for them to aspire to. If you're leading a team of entrepreneurial misfits through the tribulations of starting a company, map out what they can expect and define what success looks like.

ATTENTION. When a conductor stands with the baton raised, every eye is locked on him or her. Command attention in the same way, with gestures, eye contact, and expectant silence. You are the authority figure.

GENEROSITY. Each orchestral player knows that if they do their jobs well, they will have a moment to shine. That makes it okay for them to submit to the conductor's lead. When you have your people's attention and have established your authority, be sure to give each person multiple opportunities to demonstrate their other gifts.

As author and preacher Max Lucado said, "A man who wants to lead the orchestra must turn his back on the crowd."

33

TURN YOUR COIN INTO A BUNNY

Positioning expert Mark Levy is lots of things: our friend and mentor, an accomplished author, and a tenth-level kung fu master of persuasion. His firm, Levy Innovation, teaches consultants and thought leaders how to break down their restrictive ways of thinking about what they do, reposition themselves in powerful ways, and dramatically boost their fees. His bestsellers *Accidental Genius: Using Writing to Generate Your Best Ideas, Insight, and Content* (2000) and *How to Persuade People Who Don't Want to Be Persuaded* (with coauthor Joel Bauer, 2004) are must reads for anyone with a brain.

Levy is also an accomplished amateur magician and was a "magic consultant" for the 1997 book *Magic for Dummies* by his friend David Pogue and worked as creative director for magician Steve Cohen's show *Chamber Magic*. So he knows a thing or two about persuasion, shaping how people respond to stimuli, and the tricks that can help them radically transform their thinking to their own benefit. We sat down with Levy to talk about persuasion, and he gave us a master class on something we hadn't thought about before: the power of letting people see how you change one thing into another.

› Let People See the Show

"All the ways that I try to persuade people, they're all open and ethical and honest," Levy says about persuasion in the workplace. "One of the techniques I talk about is the 'open kitchen' concept of persuasion. Years ago, if you were building a restaurant, where would the kitchen be? It would be in the back, and there would be big walls and swinging opaque doors. Now, if you design a new restaurant, you don't put the kitchen in the back. You put the kitchen right up front where everyone can see it."

Levy told us about a restaurant in England that inspired this concept. The first floor is the kitchen, and the diners sit on a mezzanine overlooking it so they can watch their food being prepared below. The allure of secrecy has become the allure of transparency. People want to see the show, and that's the key to captivating them.

Levy talks about this in terms of magic: "With magic, you can't do things that are too subtle. People don't appreciate it. Let's say I took a quarter out of my pocket, had you examine it, then I took the quarter and made a magic pass over it with my other hand. Then I said, 'Now look at it! The date on it *was* 2016 when we started, and *now* the date is 2017. The date changed!'" Most people would say, "Big whoop."

Wowing your audience requires more radical, theatrical transformation. It's the scope and scale of the change that blows their minds. If you turn that quarter into a bunny, Levy says, well *now* you have their attention. Show them the quarter, set off some smoke bombs, cue the drum roll, and then whip away the magic handkerchief to reveal a real live rabbit! That's how you make people say, "Wow! That's incredible!"

› Persuade the Unpersuadable

Magicians know that their audiences come to their shows ready to be awestruck. That's part of the fun. Nobody's going to lay down big money for a prime seat at a Las Vegas magic show to spend that time pointing and shouting, "I see the wires! I see the wires!" Most people want a magician to transport them, just for a few minutes, to a state where they can lay down their cynicism and *believe.* One of the best examples of this happened in 1983 when David Copperfield made the Statue of Liberty disappear on live TV. It was pretty awesome, and what was most awesome about it was that a live audience was seated on a stage on Liberty Island, and even *they* were fooled.

But were they, really? The secret of the trick was kept quiet for decades, but now it's come out. Turns out that the platform the people and cameras were on actually *rotated.* When the lights on the statue were turned out, everything turned imperceptibly about twenty degrees: the audience, the cameras, the tall towers that held the giant curtain that hid the statue from view. The TV helicopters hovering overhead moved, too. When the curtain was dropped, gasp! Lady Liberty was gone . . . because the audience and cameras were now pointed a little to her left. Pretty damned clever.

We know what you're thinking, because we thought the same thing. *How could the people sitting on the platform not notice that it was turning?* Simple. They wanted to be fooled. They wanted to believe, for just a second.

That's how you persuade those unpersuadable people: you make them *want* to be persuaded.

› How to Own This Mantra

This Mantra is all about the art of transformation—showing the before and after—to wow people.

The big thing is that you can't be subtle. People want to be dazzled, so dazzle them by dialing up the drama. This is why shows like *Fixer Upper* on HGTV are so fascinating. Rare Breeds Chip and Joanna Gains take the most dilapidated property on the block and turn it into a showstopper. Without wheeling apart that life-size poster of the haggard old home to reveal the gorgeous new one, the renovated home just wouldn't seem as extraordinary. Seeing the transformation from mundane to miraculous is what blows the audience away.

To do that, adhere to the three stages of a magic trick, courtesy of the film *The Prestige*:

ACT 1: THE PLEDGE. This is when a magician shows the audience something ordinary. Like the coin. Like the run-down houses Chip and Joanna show to their clients. You're setting expectations—establishing the basis for comparison to what you're about to do.

ACT 2: THE TURN. The magician takes the ordinary and makes it extraordinary. This is when Joanna shows the client the new design plan that will turn the ugly property into their dream house. It's also where they power through all the trials and tribulations and overcome the obstacles of the renovation.

ACT 3: THE PRESTIGE. This is where Rare Breeds shine. The big reveal. Your audience was *expecting* you to make the ordinary into something extraordinary, and you did. You've just turned the coin into a bunny and wowed them with the change. But you're not done. Although they're delighted, they knew it was coming, so you haven't totally surprised them. That's why you do something *extra*, like Chip and Joanna do when they sneak a secret gift made just for the client into the impeccably designed final masterpiece and leave them with the cherry on top.

Beauty influencer Farah Dhukai lures in an audience of 6.5m Instagram followers by showing dramatic before and after photos of her personal metamorphosis. Now it's your turn to hook people with your ability to create magical transformation.

34

LEAVE ROOM FOR MAGIC

Once upon a time, there was a wildly charismatic, sensual, and mischievous philosopher, mathematician, physicist, and scientist named Émilie du Châtelet. She was born in 1706, and to say that she was an overachiever would be an understatement. By age twelve, she spoke six languages. She had an affair with Voltaire and wrote a book with him (though, typical for the time, only he got credit). She entered a contest sponsored by the French Academy of Sciences that asked "What is fire?," and her essay "Dissertation sur la nature et la propagation du feu" has become a scientific classic. She translated Isaac Newton's *Principia* and even contributed something new to Newtonian mechanics: a postulated conservation law for total energy.

Now, *that's* a story.

However, like all women who were ahead of their time, much of du Châtelet's story is not known. That's more than sad, because she was a gifted polymath who was the equal of the most brilliant (male) scientists of her day. It falls to us to tell her story, and that highlights an important truth:

Stories don't matter if they're not told.

We all have a story. You do. Your work does. If you're leading or running an organization, it has a story. That story fills in the many details that can't always be found on Instagram or in a tweet: how you got where you are, what you stand for, what you care about, what you find funny. But telling a story isn't just about sharing information or even entertaining people.

Storytelling is one of the most potent tools you have for growing your reputation or brand. By framing who you are, what you do, and why you do it in terms of a story, you shape how people perceive you. You invite them in. You influence how they feel, but in a way that makes them feel involved and valued, not manipulated.

By telling an origin story filled with drama and conflict, crushing defeats and soaring victories, you capture the imagination of your audience and help them see you as something special . . . as a Rare Breed. Would we care as much about Toms Shoes, which gives a pair of shoes to a needy child for each pair purchased, if we didn't know that founder Blake Mycoskie started the company after he witnessed the hardships children face growing up without shoes in Argentina?

A great story is like alchemy. It gives the storyteller, the hypnotic Rare Breed, the power to transmute the common and humdrum into the remarkable. That's why it's so important to make room in your professional activities to tell your story and weave an enchantment. Your story can also inspire others to support what you do. So find your story, develop it, and tell it often to whoever will listen.

› The Heist Tale

Heist's story is pretty simple: the company launched in 2015 because women's tights sucked. They ladder, sag, and bunch around the waist until even the sveltest of us look like we're jammed into a bunch of sausage casing. Heist's founders said, "Screw that. Women deserve to wear something pretty and comfortable that doesn't cost $200 a pair or make them look like they're tardy for Catholic elementary school."

Science, meet tights. Coming from outside the luxury apparel world, Heist's founders didn't know which rules they couldn't break in designing their products, so they broke them all. After a year of reimagining, 197 samples, and some 3D manufacturing, they had designed a line of stylish, comfortable, affordable tights that women would kill for. One problem: nobody knew who Heist was. That's where storytelling comes in.

As Heist chief executive Toby Darbyshire recalled in an interview with the *Guardian,* "My spark came [in 2015], walking through the London underground and coming across a very traditional underwear ad, picturing a woman in suspenders and heels standing in a library. I thought: 'Hang on a second, is this really how this industry talks to its customers?'" So Heist flipped the script and told a different story, not one of fetishized woman for the male gaze, but something to push our culture's taboo button on what women's body parts should look like. So the company designed an ad campaign for the London Underground that featured real women wearing Heist tights while buck naked from the waist up. Only the women's backs were visible, but London Transport still demanded that they be covered up.

Jackpot. The press jumped on the controversy and just like that, Heist was famous. It was changing the narrative about women's bodies and leaned in to it: the second ad campaign put fruit and vegetables—watermelon, eggplant, pear—into Heist tights to promote body positivity. Its strategy to challenge conventional scripts and give a new story for its product turned an unknown brand into a sensation.

› How to Own This Mantra

Heist's founders knew they had no chance of breaking through if they went for the hard sell. They didn't have the money, and the competition was too entrenched. But when they told a different story, with women's bodies for the female gaze as the main character, they jumped the line and became a phenomenon.

Sometimes there's strategy behind storytelling. You want to pull your customers closer, gain their empathy, or make it clear what you or your business stand for. Other times, storytelling is about nothing more than creating delight.

For example, London's Cutter & Squidge bakery has won fans from around the world by turning its tea room into a Harry Potter–esque "potion room." Patrons can don a cloak before proceeding down a dark corridor into a room straight out of Hogwarts, with brick archways, candles, flasks, and flagons and a fireplace with a cauldron over a low flame. A ticket gets you a seat at a "potions class" where you learn to make witches' brews and then eat traditional English goodies. That's using physical, environmental, sensual storytelling to make people smile and light up their day. (We want to go!)

Storytelling is ancient, organic magic that's been happening since the first humans sat around a fire, surrounded by the great, dark night, and one of them said, "Once upon a time . . ." Using it is like casting a charm spell, winning people over to your side because they see a facet of you they didn't know about before. Storytelling lets you reshape reality to suit your goals.

The first thing you must do to put this Mantra to work is to figure out what your story is. How did you get where you are? Why do you do what you do? Telling your story lends context to your brand and lets people feel like they know you—like you're something more than a logo and a price list. It tells your listeners about your character, what matters to you, and what you have in common with them.

Once you know what your story is, figure out how to tell it. We usually advise our clients to share it everywhere, from speeches to packaging to their websites. Take it a step further and let your story shape the space you work in, a retail environment, or your physical appearance. If your story is captivating and powerful, sprinkle it over everything you do like fairy dust. Let it become the mythology of your business.

Here are some rules to great storytelling:

GREAT STORIES ARE UNIVERSAL. They speak to big, human-centered topics that the audience can relate to (things like birth, growth, adversity, aspirations, conflicts).

GREAT STORIES LOVE THE UNDERDOG. The time you and your partners lived in your cars for the first two months of your startup because you were so broke, and how one morning you all woke up and you'd been towed? Pure gold. Customers and the press love a good underdog story filled with sacrifice, hard work, and winning.

GREAT STORIES MAKE THE OLD NEW AGAIN. Very little is new. No matter how original you think your brand, design, or message is, people have almost certainly experienced something like it before. But your story is unique, because nobody has lived your life. No one else is you. Lean in to what makes your story remarkable. That's how you leave room for magic.

GREAT STORIES ARE SENSORY. They create clear images in people's minds. They make them feel the blades of grass. Taste the salty oyster. Feel the hot rain pelting down on the pavement as they run through the streets of San Francisco.

VIRTUE 7

EMOTIONAL

Sensitive. Intuitive. Compassionate. Sentimental. Vulnerable.

An asset when a sensitive heart and intuitive understanding dissolve barriers between people and create connections that wouldn't otherwise be possible.

A weakness when emotional expression isn't tempered by self-regulation, leading to naiveté, thin skin, feeling overwhelmed, and a tendency to feel easily judged, defeated, or heartbroken.

People talk about emotions in terms of the heart because the heart, not the brain, was thought to be the seat of all thinking. Ancient Egyptians believed that the heart represented the soul, intelligence, memory, feeling, and personality and that it would be judged after death. That's why they preserved the heart during mummification but threw away the brain. When a person traveled to the afterlife, the heart was presented to the gods and weighed on a scale against the feather of Ma'at, the god of truth. If the heart weighed the same as or less than the feather, that person would proceed to heaven, the fields of Hetep and Iaru. But if the heart was heavier than the feather—weighed down with lies and sin—it would be devoured by the monster Ammit, and that person would cease to exist.

And you thought *your* performance reviews were rough.

Fast forward three thousand years to modern neuroanatomy and we see things a little differently. Science started telling us that emotions are mental, electrochemical impulses from the brain's limbic system that move an organism to do things like cuddling its offspring. Well, isn't that lifeless and reductive?

In the end, however, where emotions come from doesn't matter. Emotions make us who we are, and they matter because of what they *do*. We think we're driven by reason and logic, but we're really driven by what we care about. According to the science of psychoneuroimmunology (we almost pulled a muscle with that one) our emotions affect our immune system too. Anxiety, tension, and sadness give us all sorts of ailments. If you've always thought emotions were contagious, give yourself a hug; mirror neurons in our brains help us show empathy. Research even shows that kindness can help us live longer. Knowing how to *feel* and trust feelings is an underrated superpower.

Emotion is a raw force, and Rare Breeds tend to feel emotions with greater intensity than the average person. They can't help but wear their hearts on their sleeves. So it's important to know how to manage those feelings and instincts so they can be assets, not a slippery slope. Emotional Rare Breeds have high emotional intelligence, or EQ—the ability to understand emotions and be aware of their effects so they can make emotions work for them, not against them.

> Sensitive people either love deeply or they regret deeply. There really is no middle ground because they live in passionate extremes.
>
> —Shannon L. Alder

› Rejecting "Emotional" as a Negative Word

It's too bad that society tends to label emotions—at least, acknowledging and showing them—as weakness. Our world still largely discourages us from displaying our emotions. Multiply that by ten in the professional and business arenas. If you're female and you let your emotions out, you're "being a woman." Do it as a man and you're an utter wuss. Even in creative fields like the arts where we're supposed to bare our souls, emotions are okay in *theory*, but in reality, emotional displays are often judged harshly and frowned upon. Instead of people complimenting your ability to open up, they shame or shun you for doing so. That leads many people to bottle up their emotions in a sad masquerade to appear strong and in control; but when they do that, they kill the connection to the people around them. They don't say what they need to. They fail to show up as who they really are. And they become more and more isolated.

You know the struggle, too. There's a sweet unguardedness and wide-eyed innocence to you. Every Christmas, you feel an ache in your heart where your belief in Santa used to be. You're the first one to hug a colleague after a bad breakup. And sometimes, you hate being this way. You're filled with compassion, kindness, and care because that's how you're wired, but you also absorb people's pain and disappointments as if they were your own. You're everyone's shoulder to cry on, and a dumping ground for everyone else's baggage, which can be exhausting and overwhelming.

People tell you "You're too emotional," "Don't take things so personally," and "You're too sensitive." Even today, when you're alone at your desk, you wonder whether you're cut out for business or life as an entrepreneur, leader, or change agent. Are you too sensitive to succeed? Too open? Do you *feel* too much?

On the plus side, you have profound thoughts. You already know your feelings are mighty things. You're a bridge-builder and an encourager, a bringer of light on dark days, a friend and coach and confidant—and those are *strengths*. Business, academia, technology, and the arts are all human enterprises, and nothing enhances them more than your radical humanity. Caring, respect, being mindful of other people's feelings . . . these are all qualities that will inspire people to follow you, fund you, or buy what you're selling.

Do you get your hopes up when everybody else is trying to stay cool? Check. Do you feel every cruelty like it's being inflicted on someone you love? Good. You're motivated to make things better. You're about heart and soul, not just brains and muscle.

> The best and most beautiful things in the world cannot be seen nor even touched, but just felt in the heart.
>
> **—Helen Keller, letter to Rev. Phillips Brooks,**
> ***The Story of My Life***

› It's a Beautiful Day in the Neighborhood

Elaine Aron, a psychologist who has spent decades studying what she calls "highly sensitive people," has written that such people tend to be intuitive visionaries, more aware of the needs of others, loyal, conscientious, grounded, focused, highly creative, and great leaders. We doubt there's a better testament to that, or a better ambassador for the incredible power of pure, simple niceness, than the late Fred Rogers.

If you're older than about thirty, you probably saw *Mister Rogers' Neighborhood* firsthand, but if you never have, let us explain why its host embodies everything we're talking about here. *Mister Rogers' Neighborhood* was a children's show on PBS that ran from 1968 to 2001, and although it was low-tech and ultra-dorky, it was also astonishingly wonderful. At a time when kids' shows ran the gamut from *He-Man and the Masters of the Universe* to *ThunderCats* to brainless clown acts, Fred Rogers proudly led with his heart and his feelings. He was attentive and respectful to the emotions of others; that was his greatest strength. He spoke to children quietly and courteously about how it was okay to be scared or mad, and about being kind and brave.

But what really made Mr. Rogers so extraordinary was the fact that he was just like the character he portrayed on his show. And like his character, the real Fred Rogers knew that emotion, when understood, nurtured, and shared, is a powerful tool for changing minds. The nation saw just how powerful on May 1, 1969, when Rogers appeared on television before a Senate subcommittee to defend PBS from proposed budget cuts. In that room filled with cynical politicians and journalists, his sincerity and heartfelt honesty were like a lighthouse in the dark. Here's part of what he said:

> This is what I give. I give an expression of care every day to each child, to help him realize that he is unique. I end the

> program by saying, "You've made this day a special day, by just your being you. There's no person in the whole world like you, and I like you, just the way you are." And I feel that if we in public television can only make it clear that feelings are mentionable and manageable, we will have done a great service for mental health.

Subcommittee chairman Senator John Pastore, as hard-bitten as anyone in the room, responded with, "I'm supposed to be a pretty tough guy, and this is the first time I've had goose bumps for the last two days." And after Rogers finished his testimony (and even recited a poem and sang a song), Pastore said, "Looks like you just earned the 20 million dollars."

Now, if you'll pardon us for a second, we've, ahem, got something in our eyes.

> People have said, "Don't cry" to other people for years and years, and all it has ever meant is, "I'm too uncomfortable when you show your feelings. Don't cry." I'd rather have them say, "Go ahead and cry. I'm here to be with you."
>
> —**Fred Rogers**

› Leading with Heart

Surely all this touchy-feely gibberish stops when you take a leadership position in a company or a team, right? Leading others, whether it's a group of five or one hundred thousand, is about cutthroat competition, pressure, teamwork, and getting things done. There's no place for sentimental softies, is there?

Think again. Sensitive types aren't inherently disadvantaged—they are emotionally intuitive. Branson admits to relying on it. Jobs and Gates have both depended on it. Oprah credits much of her success to it. Countless other gifted leaders have used this enigmatic, largely misunderstood sixth sense to guide the way.

The ability to understand something immediately, without the need for conscious reasoning, and then make key decisions amid a forest of ever-changing external information and differing opinions is vital. Your intuition allows you to think ahead of the curve and orient yourself without having to rest on spreadsheets or gather piles of data to tell you what to do or where to go.

Our experiences working with organizations of all shapes and sizes have shown us that companies helmed by emotional leaders have tremendous advantages over their competition. Their company culture, how they hire, how their people talk to and treat each other—everything's different. Emotional leaders project a unique energy into an organization. Their people tend to be more engaged and invested. They care about more than their paychecks. In fact, they'll walk through fire for each other. It's really moving to see.

In contrast, leaders with no emotional connection to their people, who are driven only by results or wielding authority, usually end up building stone cold organizations. Their employee turnover is high (and just as expensive), they have zombie cultures, and they operate without vision or purpose. There's no humanity in them, and you can feel it. Walk down the halls and ask people, "What do you like about working here?" and you'll be answered with blank stares. People are marking time and working for the weekend.

In 2005, Jubilant FoodWorks, the exclusive Domino's Pizza franchisee in India, was on the verge of failure. A new CEO, with no experience in food service, came in to turn things around. By 2015,

India was Domino's second largest market. How did the CEO, Ajay Kaul, do it? He focused on the emotional connection between employees, customers, and the brand. He gave every employee his cell number. He started conducting monthly surveys of employee and customer happiness. Whenever a driver left to deliver pizzas in the chaotic streets of Mumbai or Delhi, every employee would shout, "Drive safely!" in a kind of verbal group hug. It was sweet, kind, and incredibly effective.

When things go wrong, emotional Rare Breeds take the heat, but when things go well, they give all the credit to their team. They know the names and family members of everyone, down to the custodians and security guards. They're not too important to clean the break room, and they never forget to celebrate you for a job well done.

Of all the companies we've worked with, we can count on the fingers of one hand the true heart-centric leaders who've built organizations based on sincerity, vulnerability, respect, and love. When you're leading a company or a team with your heart, that's your edge. You don't fear feelings and you don't fear being seen as emotional. You use vulnerability to inspire others and set yourself apart as someone who cares about people, respects how people feel, and walks the walk.

> We are all a people in need
> We are not perfect. We are not machines.
> We make mistakes.
> We need grace. We need compassion.
> We need help at times.
> We need other people.
> And that's okay.
>
> —Jamie Tworkowski, *If You Feel Too Much*

› The Dark Side of Emotion (a Blessing and a Curse)

The dark side of this Virtue is bound up in two words: *naiveté* and *fragility*. Let's start with the first. While being emotional makes you a force for good, going too far can make you a target for unscrupulous people who can and will take advantage of you. The sentiment "Nice guys finish last," attributed to pugnacious baseball manager Leo Durocher, isn't completely wrong.

The harsh reality of the world is that not all people in it are good ones, and it's important not to let empathy and optimism blind you to the need for skepticism, confidentiality, and a "prove it to me" mindset. There's nothing hypocritical about wanting someone to vet their credentials. Being naive and thinking that everyone in the world cares about you is a sure way to end up on your ass. You'll wonder how the private equity guys who invested in your company just took it away from you, how the job interview you thought you nailed shockingly went to someone else, or how that upstart competitor stole your best client.

As for fragility, it is possible you can feel too much and become overwhelmed by the Midtown Manhattan speed and stakes of life and business that you are left feeling hopeless. You can feel misunderstood a lot, and you experience heartbreak to the extreme. This can lead to harsh self-criticism, loneliness, negativity, complaining, and a dark cloud hanging over your head. On top of that, you put other people's needs in front of your own. Don't force your tender psyche into a field that's too punishing for it. That's not cowardice. That's self-awareness, and emotional Rare Breeds have plenty of that.

Here's what we've found: Empaths and emotionally sensitive people are gifts in this crazy world. Yes, you can be misunderstood, but you also make an extraordinary nurturer, confidant, and friend. So if this sounds like you, raise your emotional antenna even higher—you have so much to give.

› Three Ways to Build Your Emotional Tool Kit

Emotionally sensitive people are more in tune than the average person on the street. They're hyperaware, tuned in to a different frequency, and have copious amounts of EQ. So if that's you, before we move to the Mantras, three pieces of advice:

1. FIND YOUR OPPOSITE NUMBER.

One of the hallmarks of emotional people is self-awareness; you know your weaknesses. That means knowing that as an emotionally charged person, you have the potential to be too trusting or even to be taken advantage of. So maybe it's a good idea to find a second-in-command whose skepticism, black-and-white nature, and cold love of the facts can balance your hypersensitivity.

2. TRUST YOUR GUT.

For a long time, science wasn't even aware of the role of our unconscious. Studies now show that only 20 percent of the brain's gray matter is dedicated to conscious thoughts, while 80 percent is nonconscious thoughts. These nonconscious thoughts accelerate decision-making in the form of intuitions, hunches, and gut feelings. As an emotional

Rare Breed, use instinct and intuition to connect to your surroundings. This doesn't mean you shouldn't also be extremely level-headed, but it does mean you're willing to go with your gut even if it conflicts with supporting data.

3. PROTECT YOURSELF.

You have great insight and instinct, which means people often come to you for advice and words of encouragement. They don't know how much energy it drains from you to be a good listener, and some people take your listening for granted. You'll want to give yourself at least one day a week when you shut it down and do something for only yourself. Make sure you have a safe space where you can rest and recharge your tired soul.

The following Mantras are like love notes made of people who have found the courage to lead with their feelings first. Their stories are warm and poignant, and in the end, they will inspire you as much as they inspired us. May they hug you like a friend.

35

THE ANSWER IS IN THE QUESTION

Back in the quiet, boring days before the interwebs, possibly around the time the Magna Carta was signed, there were people called advice columnists. They were world-famous, with pen names like Abigail Van Buren and Ann Landers. People seeking solutions to problems about family, work, and relationships could write to major newspapers of the time asking for advice from "Dear Abby" or "Ask Ann Landers." That's right, a handwritten note stuck in an envelope, slurped shut with a bit of spit, and then mailed. Gasp. The columnists would publish their responses for everyone to read.

Newspapers are almost quaint relics of the past, but advice columnists aren't. Eccentric and outspoken journalist E. Jean Carroll has written her "Ask E. Jean" column for *Elle* magazine since 1993. The secret to her longevity? She doesn't pretend to know everything or have all the answers. But she does know one thing: she doesn't need to impart some sort of special wisdom to her readers, because in her opinion they already know what they need to know. In other words, you need only to look within.

"The answer is in their question," she says. "You just find out what they want to do and then you tell them to do it." What makes E. Jean a grade-A emotional Rare Breed is that she knows how to channel her gift of intuition and emotional intelligence to interpret what her readers need and give them the right advice.

The formidable Carroll dislikes anything that gets in the way of self-awareness, including dating technology, which she despises. In fact, she's developed a dating app parody called Damn Love. The object is simple and deliciously evil: break up the imaginary couples by answering a series of questions in a way that causes maximum relationship damage. We'd expect nothing less from her.

She isn't giving generic advice or wildly random feedback; she's giving people a reminder of what they already know deep down to be true. One saucy 2018 column, written in response to a woman who was lamenting that her boyfriend's crush on Scarlett Johansson was killing their sex life, illustrates exactly what she means:

> Please. *Of course* he has a crush on Scarlett Johansson. If Scarlett Johansson and the U.S. Congress were trapped in a burning building, *everybody* would save Scarlett first. So ask yourself one question: WWSD? What *Would* Scarlett Do with a chap who refused to bang her?
>
> Right. Your first reaction is the correct answer.

In other words, stop being your own worst enemy and start trusting yourself. E. Jean's keenly attuned emotional radar lets her look past what people *say* to perceive what they *mean*.

› How to Own This Mantra

Many moons ago in distant lands and ancient cultures, humans relied on their inner voices to govern their lives. In today's modern world, there are so many voices piping up in our heads, they drown out the one meaningful voice we most often need to hear: our own.

Forget about data, algorithms, or artificial intelligence. No computer can tell you what's in your own heart or convey the layers of meaning behind your words. Fortunately, your instincts are all you need to know what to do. As E. Jean Carroll says, if you really listen to the questions, you'll find that you probably already know most of the answers.

Often, we ask questions not because we don't know the answers but because we want validation. We want someone else to say, "You're right. You should quit and go out on your own," or "I think moving to the Belize jungle is a terrific idea!"

In order to tap in to why you're asking certain questions, try analyzing various cues. For example:

- What's really underneath this question?
- What's driving me to find the answer?
- What's tripping me up right now?
- Why do I feel stuck?
- What isn't sitting well with me about this person or situation?
- Do I feel conflicted?
- Am I living in alignment with my values (purpose, goals, happiness, etc.)?

Remember, your intuitive radio station doesn't broadcast consistently, and it certainly doesn't keep regular hours. You've got to tune in.

36

SHOW TEETH

Reese Witherspoon's friend Kerry Washington describes Witherspoon's personal style as "genteel Southern badass," and that's not a bad way to sum up the woman herself. Witherspoon has been in the public eye since at least the late 1990s, when she starred in *Pleasantville*, but in recent years she's become a force in Hollywood as the producer of hit films like *Gone Girl* and the HBO drama series *Big Little Lies*. But her latest role—leading the fiercely optimistic fight to put women's storytelling voices on an equal footing with men's—may be her most important.

Witherspoon's weapon of choice for doing this is her fast-growing production company, Hello Sunshine. She and her team have been gobbling up the rights to hot novels by female authors, with plans to do something that, in the words of *Fast Company* writer Mary Kaye Schilling, hasn't been done before: "build a premium independent film and TV studio within a direct-to-consumer, female-led brand that operates on multiple platforms."

With her venture, Witherspoon is doing what we call "showing teeth"—being emotionally fearless in protecting your territory or going after what you want. She says that as she aged past her perky self in *Election*, meaty roles were hard to find, something that plagues all women in Hollywood. "It was getting laughable how bad the parts were, particularly for women over 35," she says in *Fast Company*. "And that, of course, is when you become really interesting as a woman."

Armed with brains, talent, and a passion for stories by and about women, Witherspoon is one example of how emotional Rare Breeds show teeth. Another is Taylor Swift. As a superstar who never seems to leave the public eye, Swift is a popular target for brutal gossip about her exes, her posse, her control of her image—pretty much everything. And in her 2017 smash hit record, *Reputation*, and the record-breaking tour that followed it, she clapped back at every critic and everyone who's thrown shade or misunderstood her.

Even the album's cover is a shot across the bow at the media. Newspaper articles are superimposed over half of Swift's face, sending a clear message: *What you write about me is only half the story.* The tracks themselves throw daggers at former lovers who think they're saving her, the reality of being a star, the critics and haters, and her own wink-wink manipulation of all of the above. *You think you know me, but you don't. You think you own me, but I'm really in control here.*

In the wild, an animal that bares its teeth is warning its potential enemies that whatever is nearby is too close. And if attacked, it will stand its ground and fight back. By showing your teeth, you're telling your aggressor, *You really don't want a piece of this.*

When you act assertively to defend yourself, your brand, your intellectual property, or your reputation, you'll accomplish three important things. First, you'll let everyone else know you're someone they shouldn't fuck with. It's a cutthroat world, and a little healthy fear discourages people from messing with you or stealing what's yours. Second, showing teeth attracts people who respect your guts and style and want to work with you.

And third, there's an old saying: "The best defense is a good offense." By stepping up to a confrontation instead of backing away from it, you'll make others react to you. You become the "alpha," the leader, the dominant presence. That gives you the floor and puts you in control of the narrative.

› The Bite of Serena Williams

Case in point: tennis superstar Serena Williams's emotion-laden tirade at the 2018 French Open. Williams has always been outspoken and provocative, and she had already sparked headlines at the Open by wearing a form-fitting black catsuit that was subsequently banned.

During the final match, frustrated by the actions of umpire Carlos Ramos, who penalized her for receiving hand signals from her coach in the stands, the GOAT in women's tennis threw down on the court. She called Ramos a thief, smashing her racket in a fit of anger and screaming, "You owe me an apology!" Williams continued to stalk Ramos, was penalized more than once, and ended up losing the match. Critics accused her of upstaging her opponent, Naomi Osaka, during the younger player's first Grand Slam win. People saw it as unsportsmanlike conduct—a complete, raging teenage meltdown.

But there was a lot more to that emotional on-court outburst than met the eye. Granted, Williams took the bait, but it wasn't a petty fight; it was an impassioned defense. Williams showed her teeth and announced to the tennis world that she was done tolerating sexism against women—something that's been a problem in pro tennis for a long time. At the post-tournament press conference, she told reporters that she was fighting for women's equality in tennis. About Ramos she said, "He's never taken a game from a man because they said 'thief.' For me, it blows my mind. But I'm going to continue to fight for women." It wasn't about winning or showing up her opponent; it was about defending herself, *and* other women players. In fact, when the trophies were handed out, Williams was the peacemaker, asking the booing crowd to celebrate Osaka for her win.

In showing teeth, Williams served notice that she would no longer be silent in the face of unfair treatment of women. She was also issuing a direct challenge to the perception that when a woman of color stands up and speaks her mind, she's a threat. Her message was clear: *You won't bully me.*

› How to Own This Mantra

Showing teeth is about guarding yourself and others when necessary. It can be a warning sign, or it can be a vigorous protection. It can also extend to smaller acts, like protecting your family, business, culture, team, or colleagues.

Work to establish a reputation as someone ethical and no-nonsense and who fights for what they believe in. How? Simple. Deliver best-in-class results, act fairly and honorably, work hard, and never let anyone push you around. That means learning to *frame* threats in a productive way. What do we mean? Well, what you take from the events of your life depends on how you choose to perceive them—how you frame what happened. You can choose to see a threat as a reminder of a time you were hurt or helpless, or you can see it as evidence that something extraordinary happened to you and you survived, stronger and wiser.

The concept of *learned helplessness*, which the psychologists Martin Seligman and Steven Maier started researching in the late 1960s, is all about this kind of thinking. In their early experiments, they showed that a dog, expecting an electrical shock after hearing a tone, eventually stopped trying to avoid the shock. The same thing can happen with people: when you feel you have no control over a situation, you feel helpless and stop trying to make changes or look for opportunities. You choose to see a negative event as something that you caused and as a judgment of your capabilities, so you can permanently disable your will to try to achieve. But if you choose to see a failure or disappointment as something that could have happened to anyone—something you'll shake off and learn from—you train yourself to be more optimistic and confident.

Look at a recent threat that wounded you. How did you define it in the moment? (Probably something like "This sucks," we'd guess.) But now, with hindsight, how could you define, or frame, it in a way that empowers you instead of making you feel small or weak? You might be able to see what happened as a lesson, or a test. You might find that you can use that feeling and that experience constructively. If you reframe and redefine the situation, you probably will feel differently about yourself.

In the future, try to reframe situations when you come up against a threat and empower yourself rather than risk "learning helplessness" and feeling that you can't avoid such a situation again.

37

WRITE LOVE LETTERS

A lot of people were outraged at Howard Schultz, former chairman and CEO of Starbucks, when he announced he might run for president as an independent. But even if you were one of them, you have to admit that the guy has the courage to wear his heart on his sleeve. He's famous for the honest, deeply felt letters he wrote to Starbucks partners, like this excerpt from the one he wrote when he announced his departure in June 2018:

> Dear Starbucks partners—past and present,
>
> I write to you today enjoying a French Press of my favorite coffee, aged Sumatra, and feeling so many emotions. Pride. Nostalgia. A heavy heart. But mostly, I sit here feeling a tremendous sense of gratitude. For years I've had a dream to build a different kind of company, one that has the potential to enhance lives and endure long after I was gone. Thanks to you, my dream has come true. . . .
>
> I believe in my heart that Starbucks partners will continue what was started decades ago. Great coffee and our stores will always be

catalysts for community. Now more than ever the world needs places to come together with compassion and with love. Providing the world with a warm and welcoming third place may just be our most important role and responsibility, today and always.

Onward with love,

Howard

What billionaire CEO closes his emails with "Onward with love"? Only Schultz. That's how he's always operated, and the success of Starbucks shows that his servant leadership style works. From asking baristas to scrawl race-conscious messages on coffee cups to his genuinely agonized response after two black men were arrested at a Starbucks in Philly in 2018, he knows that when people feel they can relate to a company on an emotional level, both the company and its customers thrive.

Some cynics scoff at Schultz's approach, but don't they always when leaders reject traditional testosterone-drenched power tactics for real feelings? Being a sensitive, intuitive, caring leader—especially at the helm of one of the world's most iconic brands—takes guts. That's what makes Schultz such a Rare Breed: he leverages his emotions, embraces them, and lets them work to his favor. Schultz has admitted that while he often relied on data while sitting in the CEO's chair, he's always relied more on his empathy and sense of what's right.

› How to Own This Mantra

Get out your fountain pen or open a blank email and let people know how you feel. Heartfelt letters can go a long way to calm concerns, lift spirits, rally your organization, and create a connection. It's a sacred act to do this, and one that's undervalued. Here are some thoughts for you to consider:

CONFRONT THE ELEPHANTS. If your company or team is going through tough or shifting times, don't duck, hedge, or waffle about the problems. Acknowledging issues is necessary in order to move through them. If you've made poor hiring decisions, admit it. If you haven't been the best leader you can be, say so. Put words to the underlying sentiment, but move quickly from the problem to the solution to keep everyone moving forward.

EXPRESS GRATITUDE. One of William Arthur Ward's inspirational truths is, "Feeling gratitude and not expressing it is like wrapping a present and not giving it." Praise and recognition are emotional currency. When you show your appreciation for the contributions and hard work of others, you engage people at the heart level and increase their happiness. Keeping up morale can be a difficult, but saying "thank you" makes it the easiest thing on earth.

During her time as CEO at PepsiCo, Indra Nooyi was known to write personal letters not just to her employees, but to the parents of each of the people who reported to her directly, thanking them for "the gift" of their children. Sometimes she wrote several hundred every year! The letters opened a floodgate of emotions as parents wrote back saying how deeply moved and proud they were. Nooyi embodies the Rare Breed spirit with her belief that leaders should focus on engaging people with their hearts as much as their minds in order to build loyalty and morale.

ENCOURAGE ACTION. Vision can lose significance if it's the only thing you ever talk about. Take it further and invite your team to take action. Remind them of commonalities and shared values and the fact that they have been successful in the past through tough times. Encourage tolerance, open-mindedness, and respect for one another and customers. In his 2018 letter, Howard Schultz reminded his partners to:

stay true to our reason for being: inspiring and nurturing the human spirit through a sense of community and human connection. As you adhere to our core purpose, do not forget to innovate around it. Never embrace the status quo. Instead, have the curiosity to look around corners and the courage to push for reinvention. Change is inevitable, and the world has become a more fragile place since we first opened our doors. Amid the chaos, try to listen with empathy, respond with kindness, and do your best to perform through the lens of humanity. Do not be a bystander. Instead, choose to be responsible for what you see and hear. No person or company is ever perfect, so learn from mistakes and be forgiving of yourself and others.

BE SINCERE AND UNGUARDED. A whiff of hypocrisy or insincerity, and it's game over. Reflect on what you really want to get across to your colleagues, clients, employees, or audience and make sure that what you communicate aligns with how you truly feel. It's better to say just a little than to share sentiments that aren't authentic.

KEEP THEM COMING. Writing love letters shouldn't be a once-in-a-blue-moon thing. Making it a personal ritual will be more effective. It will become something your team expects, and even looks forward to. Consider quarterly reflections for consistency, or do it ad hoc style whenever the mood strikes: to celebrate the completion of a huge project, after pulling a team all-nighter, to acknowledge outstanding customer service, or any number of small-goal wins.

38

CONTRIBUTE A VERSE

In the 1989 movie *Dead Poets Society*, English teacher John Keating (played by the late and very much missed Rare Breed Robin Williams) instructs his students to rip out a section of their textbooks that tries to break down poetry, and then he gives this spine-tingling speech (written by screenwriter Tom Schulman):

> We don't read and write poetry because it's cute. We read and write poetry because we are members of the human race. And the human race is filled with passion. And medicine, law, business, engineering, these are noble pursuits and necessary to sustain life. But poetry, beauty, romance, love, these are what we stay alive for. To quote from Whitman, "O me! O life! of the questions of these recurring; of the endless trains of the faithless, of cities filled with the foolish; what good amid these O me, O life?" Answer. That you are here—that life exists, and identity; that the powerful play goes on and you may contribute a verse. . . . What will your verse be?

Living is savage, gorgeous, and terrifying, and while we can't always experience our days as part of a single soaring epic, that is what they are. We're all living out individual, interwoven stanzas of an ode that continues to echo through the ages—one more wondrously complex than *The Waste Land*, more dramatic than *The Epic of Gilgamesh*.

But we often forget this. We get so swept away and ground down by minutiae—paying bills, answering emails, taking selfies—that we forget to step back, look around, and appreciate the wonder and awe of who we are, where we are, and what we're doing. We forget that we have the right and the *responsibility* to contribute a verse to the drama, a few notes to the great symphony of existence.

› Calling Attention to the Moment, Leaving a Legacy

Rare Breeds add something to the conversation that reminds everyone how extraordinary this moment is, how great the potential and possibility in our bodies and minds are, and how limited our time on earth is. A verse is a wake-up call to wonder, delivered through writing, music, art, dance, design, rhetoric, or the courageous act of creating a business and a brand out of an idea, determination, and hope.

We each have the privilege to determine the meaning of who we are and what we do. Your creative work, your entrepreneurial courage, your grinning rebellion—they're your verse. You have the power to exalt others, to move them to look up, to see the "powerful play," to strut center stage and recite poetry that thrills.

Poet Azure Antoinette does that. Think poetry has no place in the world of business? She disagrees. Called "the Maya Angelou of the millennial generation," she's written bespoke verse for clients like The Gap, Johnson & Johnson, and more. Organizations hire her to write and recite original poems for special events when they want to give attendees something artistic but more intimate and personal than a sculpture or a piece of classical music.

Antoinette created her career as a poet for practical reasons: she wanted to write and not starve. When we asked her how someone becomes a bespoke corporate poet, she said, "When I started doing this, I was the only person in my field!" In other words, she created her own career out of thin air, which is boss.

What we love about Antoinette is that she has built a career by doing something we all hunger to do: reach out with ideas and influence how other people think and live. She cherishes the thought that each person who hears her poems is free to find in them whatever meaning they need most. "Life is short if you're happy, but life is arduous when you don't have a purpose," she says. "The only thing I absolutely know is that I'm supposed to be creating."

No one embodies this idea better than the late Alex Calderwood. Matthew Shaer wrote of him in *Fast Company* that he was "a kind of hipster polymath" who was "able to look around the corners of culture and see what was coming years, if not decades, before everyone else." Whereas Antoinette's verse takes the form of words, Calderwood's took the form of business, disrupting an eclectic array of industries: record labels, fashion, barber shops, advertising, book publishing, hospitality experiences, and nightclubs.

But if anything epitomizes the influence of this "cultural engineer," it's the concentrated cool of his Ace Hotels chain. In breaking and then re-creating the hotel model, Calderwood infused every space, from guest rooms to common areas, with a style and substance that's hard to ignore. Ace Hotels feel like a mash-up of millennial speakeasy, co-working space, and neighborhood java joint. It seems obvious that hotels should have always been this welcoming, but it took a mind like Calderwood's—a hyperkinetic, mercurial mind for whom the whole world was Wonderland—to *make* it obvious.

Unfortunately, stars burn out. Calderwood died in 2013 at age forty-seven. However, his spirit remains in and around everything he touched. His influence still shapes how people work and what they believe to be possible.

› How to Own This Mantra

It's up to you to add something to the universe that expresses who you are in a unique way and leaves something of you behind to exalt others. Many people finish their journey without leaving behind a trace. Finding your contribution isn't just about people remembering your name; it's about people remembering what you did, how you made them feel, and what you stood for.

Worry less about what's profitable or strategically sound and focus on what your life sounds like when you write your verse with abandon.

Ryan Griffin is a Michigan barbershop owner who gives discounts to kids who read books out loud while sitting in his chair to encourage a love of books in young people. He started the Read to Your Barber Literacy Program. That's his verse.

At eighteen years old, Maggie Doyne took her life savings of $5,000 and bought land in Nepal to build a home for orphans. Kopila Valley Children's Home is now home to a community of fifty thriving children and mothers who no longer live in fear and homelessness. That's her verse.

Joshua Coombes started #DoSomethingForNothing to humanize homelessness. He gives free haircuts (plus love, hope, and kindness) to homeless people all over the world. That's his verse.

Mikaila Ulmer is a tweenage social entrepreneur and speaker who's building businesses and saving honeybees with every bottle of Me & the Bees Lemonade. That's her verse.

Find ways to contribute a verse through your business, your work, or your talent. *Rare Breed* is one of our verses. We saw something we felt could inspire readers to realize their potential, and we chose to share it. We've introduced you to singing doctors and corporate poets, so you know what's possible. Like the French poet Nicolas Boileau-Despréaux wrote in 1695, "And my verse, good or bad, always has something to say."

READ THIS LAST!

Allen Ginsberg, the revered Beat Generation poet, wrote in "Sunflower Sutra": "We're not our skin of grime . . . we're golden sunflowers inside." In other words, we're all marvelous creatures waiting to bloom. Our lives can be big, and beautiful, and full of joy. Our potential can not only be met, but fully realized.

Before we send you off on your Rare Breed journey, let us remind you: *This world needs you.* It needs passionate, fearless entrepreneurs, artists, and activists to lead us into the next generation of business, medicine, philanthropy, entertainment, and technology. It needs people who have come alive, primed for all that life has to offer. That's you.

Despite that, we know that this world might not always *deserve* you. After all, it's spent years trying to make you question whether you were broken because you're rebellious, audacious, obsessed, hot-blooded, weird, hypnotic, or emotional. Now you know better.

Here are a couple of things worth repeating: First, remember that the Virtues alone don't make you a Rare Breed. You need to use them to inspire others and build a better future. By awakening your potential, you'll make hope viral for all the gifted outliers who will follow in your footsteps.

Second, being a Rare Breed is an act of soaring, unrelenting belief. There's more to being exceptional than *wanting* to be. When it comes to launching your moonshot, you've got to believe that you have what it takes.

To the Rare Breed in you,

Sunny & Ashleigh
New York City, January 2019

ACKNOWLEDGMENTS

Writing a book is harder than we thought and more rewarding than we could have ever imagined. We were constantly caught in the tension between *Is this any good?* and *It must be perfect.* A lot of people helped push the devil off our shoulders when we were having a hard time doing it ourselves.

This book is dedicated to Sunny's parents, Crystal Bonnell and Danny Bonnell, who taught us to be good and strong, and hug like we mean it. They were (and always will be) the North Star in everything we do. Their Rare Breed spirit lives on through us.

Couldn't have done it without:

Our publisher, HarperOne, for believing in us.

Our editor, Anna Paustenbach, for making brilliant suggestions and polishing the diamond.

Our agent, Joy Tutela, for being our champion and looking after us so well.

Our writing partner, Tim Vandehey, for helping to wrangle this beast and find the right words.

Our cover designer, Matt Chase, for exploring with us and visualizing the book's essence.

Our PR and marketing friends, Mark Fortier and David Over, for your pirate-like ideas, guidance, and leadership.

Our mentor, Mark Levy, for giving us your unrelenting enthusiasm and creative genius to help bring *Rare Breed* into the world. We will always be thankful to you.

Big hugs to those who so graciously gave us their time, heard us out, and exchanged ideas:

Andrew Friedman, Peter Economy, Alexandra Levit, Alex Merry, Bob Calise, Joanne Gordon, John Funk, and Jade Burkhart.

Giant thank-yous to the Rare Breeds we interviewed:

Chef Daniel Boulud, Charlamagne Tha God, Emma Mcilroy, Kevin Kelley, Miki Agrawal, Gavin Kaysen, Johnny Earle, Chad Houser, Brian Andreas, Robert Novogratz, Cortney Novogratz, Dr. Temple Grandin, Tomi Adeyemi, and Sterling Ball.

There are hundreds more who have encouraged, inspired, supported, and given us high fives when we needed it.

Rare Breed exists because of all that love.